Antichrist
& End Times Deception

Study Outline

Introduction	3
The metallic man	4
Vision of 4 Beasts	7
The Beast System	10
1st leg - One World Religion	12
2nd Leg - Global Finance	17
3rd Leg - Rise of Antichrist	22
The Restrainer	24
Daniel's 70th week	28
Tribulation begins	31
Power struggles	32
Mid-Trib turning point	36
Abomination of desolation	39
Mark of the Beast	42
The False Prophet	43
How long oh Lord?	46
Persecutes the saints	47
Second Coming of Christ	50
Return of Christ	52
Review of beast system	54
Spirit of Antichrist is here	55
End Times deception	56
Ratio of False Prophets	59
Influence by spirits	62
Internet Prophets	64
Spiritual winds	69
Moved by winds	71
Whose voice, is it?	72
Test the spirits	74
Stand on the Word of God	76
Know God, not a religion	78
Call to Action	81
Charts	82

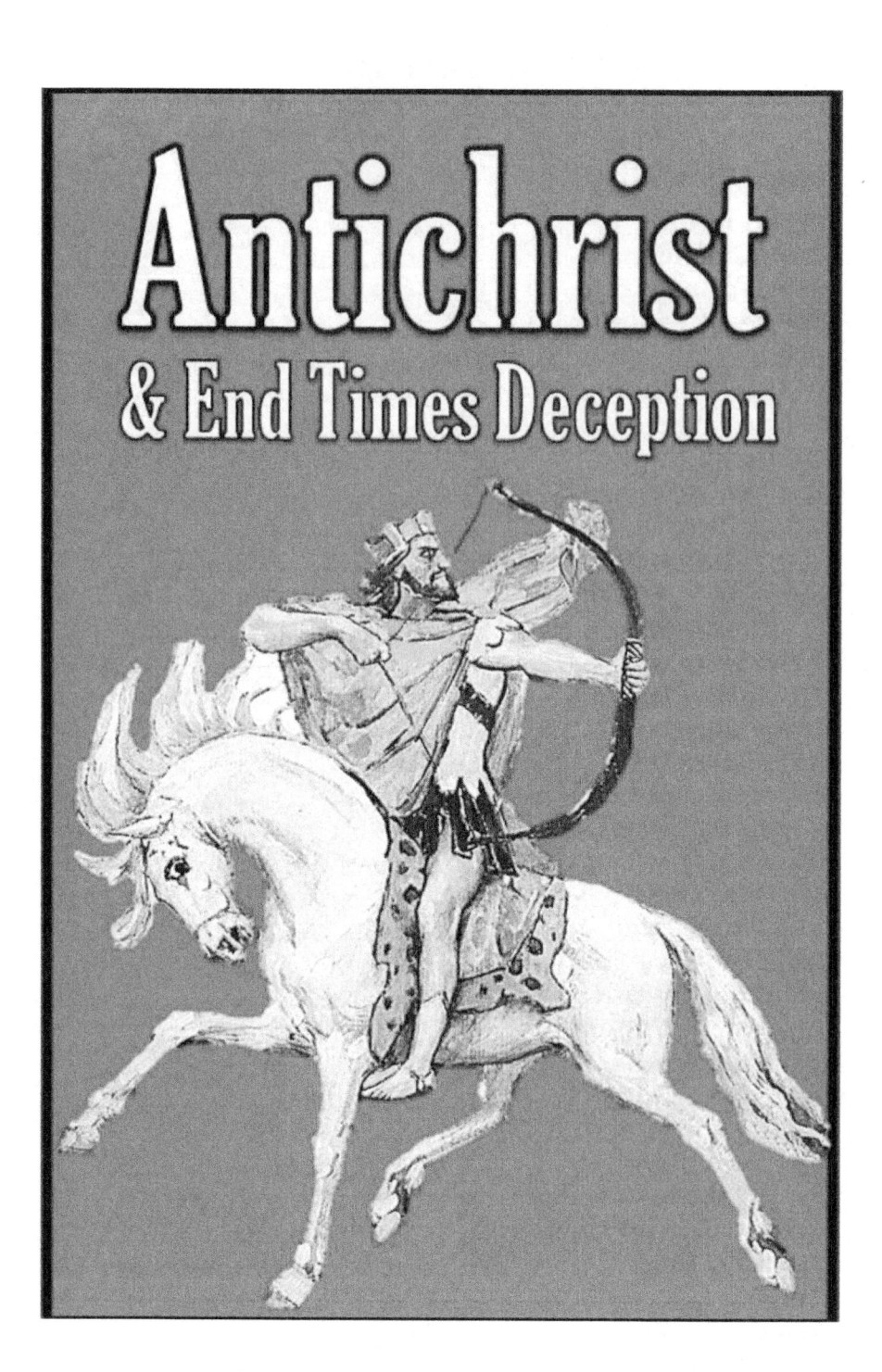

Antichrist
& End Times Deception

Antichrist
& End Times Deception

Introduction

Suppose the end times were a theater play, and we knew the script, the actors, and the scenery for each act. In that case, we would know what to expect in each scene of the play. We would know what to look for. The Bible gives us the script, and we know what to expect: forming a new world order, a global digital currency, and a state-run world religion. We know the Antichrist and false prophet are backstage, waiting to appear. Everything is getting put in place, and at any minute, the curtain could lift, and the play could start. In this book, we review the script and what to watch for.

When the disciples asked Jesus about his second coming and the signs of the end of the age, his first warning was about deception, which he repeated numerous times. Global mass deception will cover the earth in the end times, but Jesus focused his warnings for believers to be on their guard against religious frauds. Those powerful deceptions will come from false religious leaders, specifically **false prophets** and **false Christs'**, with a surge of demonically inspired teachings from the pulpits. The delusions will be so strong that even God's most zealous, discerning, and elect saints may abandon Christ and depart from the faith.

> ***Matthew 24:3-5*** *Now as He sat on the Mount of Olives, the disciples came to Him privately, saying, "tell us, when will these things be? And what will be the sign of Your coming, and of the end of the age?" And Jesus answered and said to them:* ***"Take heed that no one deceives you. "For many will come in My name, saying, 'I am the Christ,' and will deceive many.***
>
> ***Matthew 24:11*** *"Then **many false prophets will rise up and deceive many.***

*Matthew 24:24 "For **false christs and false prophets will rise and show great signs and wonders to deceive, if possible, even the elect.***

Deception is the only end-time sign that is purely mental and that war is fought continuously on the battlefield of the mind. We are a generation where artificial intelligence and algorithms try to control our minds; governments tell us what to think, and society and social platforms try to pressure us into submission to their narratives. Satanic powers and evil leaders will exploit every weakness and use every weapon to deceive and enslave people for more and more power until they have a global government. Then, a global dictator, the Antichrist, will arise; let's examine how he deceives, conquers, and rules the world for seven years.

The metallic man

The Antichrist will be the final Gentile Dictator (non-Jewish) ruling the last Gentile empire in history. We were given the history of all the Gentile empires from a dream that Nebuchadnezzar, the King of Babylon, dreamed, which was interpreted by Daniel. The king's dream was of a metallic statue of a man constructed with different metals, divided into four parts representing four Gentile empires. The metals, starting at the head with gold, go from more valuable to cheaper, from softer to harder, and weaker to stronger, representing their character.

> *Daniel 2:31-45 "You, O king, were watching; and behold, a great image! This great image, whose splendor was excellent, stood before you; and its form was awesome. 32 **"This image's head was of fine gold, its chest and arms of silver, its belly and thighs of bronze, 33 "its legs of iron, its feet partly of iron and partly of clay.***

At the end of the dream, a stone cut without hands struck the image, pulverized it, and the stone became a great mountain that filled the whole earth. The stone represents Christ at the second coming, judging and destroying the final Gentile empire. The stone becomes a mountain that fills the entire world, representing Christ, establishing the millennial kingdom, and ruling from Jerusalem.

> ***Daniel 2:34* "*You watched while a stone was cut out without hands, which struck the image on its feet of iron and clay, and broke them in pieces. 35*** *"Then the iron, the clay, the bronze, the silver, and the gold were crushed together, and became like chaff from the summer threshing floors; the wind carried them away so that no trace of them was found.* ***And the stone that struck the image became a great mountain and filled the whole earth.***

When Daniel gives the interpretation, he identifies the head of gold as Nebuchadnezzar and the Babylonian Empire.

> ***Daniel 2:31-45*** *36 "This is the dream. Now we will tell the interpretation of it before the king. 37 "You, O king, are a king of kings. For the God of heaven has given you a kingdom, power, strength, and glory; 38 "and wherever the children of men dwell, or the beasts of the field and the birds of the heaven, He has given them into your hand, and has made you ruler over them all-****you are this head of gold.***

Daniel continues to describe the second and third kingdoms, which were prophetic when Daniel spoke but are history to us. The chest and two arms of silver represent the Medo-Persian Empire. The belly and thighs represent the Empire of Greece with Alexander the Great. Daniel did not elaborate on these two kingdoms when interpreting Nebuchadnezzar's dream but gave much more information about them later, as we will see.

> *Daniel 2:31-45 39 "But after you shall arise **another kingdom** inferior to yours; **then another, a third kingdom of bronze**, which shall rule over all the earth.*

Daniel gives the most details about the fourth kingdom, which represents the Roman Empire made of iron, fierce and strong, crushing and breaking in pieces. This kingdom had two legs, representing the two capitals of the divided Empire, Rome and Constantinople (now Istanbul). There is another separation of materials of the statue; the feet and toes are iron mixed with clay, partly strong and partly fragile. The feet and toes represent a revived Roman Empire and the future Antichrist kingdom. The ten toes represent a global power distribution in ten regions with ten kings. Later, in other visions, the ten are referred to as horns, meaning powers or rulers. The mixture of iron and clay could reveal disunity in the coalition and different military and political power levels amongst the kings. We will see that the Antichrist will not ascend to dominate the Empire immediately or without resistance, manipulation, and dethroning three of the ten kings.

> *Daniel 2:40-45 "And **the fourth kingdom shall be as strong as iron**, inasmuch as iron breaks in pieces and shatters everything; and like iron that crushes, that kingdom will break in pieces and crush all the others. 41 **"Whereas you saw the feet and toes, partly of potter's clay and partly of iron, the kingdom shall be divided**; yet the strength of the iron shall be in it, just as you saw the iron mixed with ceramic clay. 42 "And as the toes of the feet were partly of iron and partly of clay, **so the kingdom shall be partly strong and partly fragile.** 43 "As you saw iron mixed with ceramic clay, they will mingle with the seed of men; but they will not adhere to one another, just as iron does not mix with clay.*

Again, part of the interpretation reveals the establishment of the millennial kingdom and the eternal kingdom of heaven that will follow that. After the destruction of the Gentile kingdoms, the statement that the kingdom will not be left to other people is a promise to the nation of Israel that they will rule over the world's final Empire until the end of time.

> **Daniel 2:40-45** *44 "And in the days of these kings **the God of heaven will set up a kingdom which shall never be destroyed; and the kingdom shall not be left to other people; it shall break in pieces and consume all these kingdoms, and it shall stand forever.** 45 "Inasmuch as you saw that the stone was cut out of the mountain without hands, and that it broke in pieces the iron, the bronze, the clay, the silver, and the gold-the great God has made known to the king what will come to pass after this. **The dream is certain, and its interpretation is sure."***

Vision of 4 Beasts

Daniel had a vision of four beasts representing the same four Gentile Empires. He saw these beasts coming out of the sea. The sea represents the sea of humanity, multitudes, the nations of peoples *(Revelation 17:15)*.

> **Daniel 7:2** *Daniel spoke, saying, "I saw in my vision by night, and behold, the four winds of heaven were stirring up the Great Sea. 3 "And **four great beasts came up from the sea**, each different from the other.*

The first beast was a winged lion, symbolizing the speed and ferocity of the Babylonian empire. The Babylonians worshipped a winged lion, which they associated with Ishtar, the goddess of fertility, love, and war. The winged lions adorn the Ishtar Gate of Babylon, which archeologists unearthed, moved, and reconstructed inside a museum in Berlin, Germany.

***Daniel 7:4** "The first was like a lion, and had eagle's wings. I watched till its wings were plucked off; and it was lifted up from the earth and made to stand on two feet like a man, and a man's heart was given to it.*

The second beast was an alliance between the Medes and Persians (modern Iran), represented by a bear with three ribs in its mouth. The three ribs represent three kingdoms they conquered: Babylon, Lydia, and Egypt. These subjugated kingdoms felt the grinding teeth of the cruel bear lording over them.

***Daniel 7:2** 5 "And **suddenly another beast, a second, like a bear. It was raised up on one side, and had three ribs in its mouth between its teeth**. And they said thus to it: 'Arise, devour much flesh!'*

The third beast was a leopard with four wings and four heads. The leopard is smaller than the lion, but the four wings made it twice as fast. The leopard represents Alexander the Great and the kingdom of Greece. Alexander came from a small kingdom and took a small force, and within twelve years, he conquered Europe, much of Asia, and the Middle East down to Egypt. Alexander died young, and his four generals divided the conquered lands between them. That explains the symbolism of the leopard having four heads.

***Daniel 7:26** "After this I looked, and there was **another, like a leopard, which had on its back four wings of a bird. The beast also had four heads, and dominion was given to it**.*

The fourth beast is "dreadful and terrible," but there are two parts to this kingdom, as we saw with the dream of the metallic man. The two legs of iron represent the historical Roman Empire. But the feet and ten toes made with iron and clay represent a future Empire from the regions where the old Roman Empire existed. That empire will have ten kings called horns, horns symbolizing power. **The ten horns on the beast in Daniel 7 represent the same thing as the ten toes on the metallic man in Daniel 2.** This power will be political and military, controlling people, regions, and resources.

*Daniel 7:7 "After this I saw in the night visions, and behold, **a fourth beast, dreadful and terrible, exceedingly strong. It had huge iron teeth; it was devouring, breaking in pieces, and trampling the residue with its feet. It was different from all the beasts that were before it, and it had ten horns**.*

Next, Daniel gives many details about the Antichrist, calling him the fourth beast or the little horn, but he will be the last Gentile dictator to dominate the world. Obtaining that power by defeating three other kings and by shrewd dealings and tactics.

*Daniel 7:8 "**I was considering the horns, and there was another horn, a little one, coming up among them, before whom three of the first horns were plucked out by the roots.** And there, in this horn, were eyes like the eyes of a man, and a mouth speaking pompous words.*

Daniel 2

Gold

Silver

Brass

Iron

Iron & Clay

Daniel 7

Babylon
605-539 BC

Medo-Persia
539-331 BC

Greece
331-168 BC

Rome
168 BC - 476 AD

The Beast System

All four Empires, represented by the beasts and metals, rose to power and fell as prophesied and are documented in history, except the unfulfilled part of the prophecy about the feet made of iron and clay with ten toes. Satan will set up that empire and turn it over to the Antichrist, who will reign for seven years. We call that time the tribulation, and the last 3 1/2 years of the seven is called the great tribulation and the time of Jacob's trouble. That will be the worst time of suffering and judgment in human history until the rock, Christ, returns and crushes that empire and establishes the millennial kingdom.

The politicians, global corporations, and elite world leaders who think they are creating a humanistic utopia are tools of the Devil to build the global government that the Antichrist will inherit. They are deceived and manipulated by their puppet master, Satan. Satan is behind the scenes, controlling the propaganda and narratives, provoking wars and famines to establish global fascism before turning over his kingdom to his man to rule the world. Notice how, in Revelation 12, the Dragon, aka Satan, has seven heads and ten horns.

> ***Revelation 12:3*** *And another sign appeared in heaven: behold,* ***a great, fiery red dragon having seven heads and ten horns, and seven diadems on his heads.*** *... **9** So the great dragon was cast out, that serpent of old,* ***called the Devil and Satan, who deceives the whole world;*** *he was cast to the earth, and his angels were cast out with him.*

Satan will perfect every evil strategy and tactic used in the previous empires, Greece the leopard, Medo Persia the bear, and Babylon the lion, and supercharges them to exercise absolute control and enslave the entire world's population. But this empire will be different than all others; it will employ modern technology. This empire will use quantum computers, artificial intelligence, and the internet to monitor and micromanage every detail of every person's life on the planet in real-time with an iron fist in a digitally surveilled concentration camp. It will be history's most controlling, powerful, and cruel dictatorship. Notice that when the Antichrist, aka the beast, rises out of the sea of humanity, he would have already taken possession of the Dragon's seven heads and ten horns, with Satan's power, throne, and great authority.

> ***Revelation 13:1*** *And I stood upon the sand of the sea, and* ***I saw out of the sea a beast coming up, having seven heads and ten horns, and upon its horns ten diadems, and upon its heads a name of evil speaking, 2 and the beast that I saw was like to a leopard, and its feet as of a bear, and its***

mouth as the mouth of a lion, and the dragon did give to it his power, and his throne, and great authority.

The beast system is like a three-legged stool; one leg is the **government** ruled by the Antichrist as commander and chief over the military, and he has ten kings over ten regions under him. The second leg is **religious**, with the false prophet forcing a coalition of the world's religions, mandating global worship of the Antichrist and his image, and killing the dissenters. The third leg is **financial**; with a fascist banking system, under the Antichrist, the global corporations and elite oligarchs will hold power in that leg. There will be a programmable global digital currency, and only those who take the mark of the beast can acquire food, housing, transportation, medical treatment, and all other services. And those who refuse to accept the mark will be killed. Let's examine the three legs: we'll start with religion, the false prophet, and the harlot church.

Babylon Mother of Harlots Antichrist One World Religion Coexist

1st leg - One World Religion
The Antichrist is called the first beast, and the false prophet is called another beast or the second beast. Both the Antichrist and false prophet get their power from Satan and forge an evil trinity, imitating and challenging God. The false prophet has a different function from the Antichrist but has the same Satanic authority as the Antichrist. He's like a lamb, meaning he imitates Christ but speaks like a dragon or Satan. Lambs don't have horns; he is a religious deceiver and does false signs by the power of Satan, and the two horns mean that he has power in two areas. The false prophet will **deceive** the world with his words and false signs, and he also has the power and authority to **kill** anyone who does not bow in worship to an image of the Antichrist.

> **Revelation 13:11** Then **I saw another beast** coming up out of the earth, and **he had two horns like a lamb and spoke like a dragon. 12 And he exercises all the authority of the first beast in his presence, and causes the earth and those who dwell in it to worship the first beast**, whose deadly wound was healed.
>
> **Revelation 13: 13 He performs great signs, so that he even makes fire come down from heaven on the earth in the sight of men. 14 And he deceives those who dwell on the earth by those signs** which he was granted to do in the sight of the beast, telling those who dwell on the earth to make an image to the beast who was wounded by the sword and lived. 15 **He was granted power to give breath to the image of the beast, that the image of the beast should both speak and cause as many as would not worship the image of the beast to be killed.**

Many believe the prime candidate to fill the office of the false prophet will be the Roman Catholic Pope. The Pope brings 1.3 billion followers to the table when he negotiates for power and brings all the world's religions together in one coalition, with him at the head. The unification process is already happening with an effort to unite the world's only monotheistic faiths that claim Abraham as their patriarch, namely Judaism (15 million), Christianity (2.6 billion), and Islam (1.8 billion). The false prophet will use Satanic signs and wonders to deceive the world into accepting the Satanic global religion.

Both Catholics and Muslims have a bloody history. Not long after Constantine and the Romans hijacked and paganized Christianity, they began to silence, torture, and kill anyone who questioned their version of religion. The Catholic priests who conducted the inquisitions were some of the most bloody and cruel torturers in history. Islam began 600 years after Christ, and from day one until now, Islam has conquered lands with bloodshed and forced conversions by the edge of the sword and acts of terrorism. The Hindus and other religions are also known to slaughter people from different faiths. We are just reporting history. Universally, most people want to live in peace, but evil religious and government leaders will do anything for power, forcing their followers to do unspeakable things. That all works perfectly well with the Harlot church, as the great whore of Babylon will be drunk with the blood of the saints, especially the last 3 1/2 years of the great tribulation.

> **Revelation 17:1** *Then one of the seven angels who had the seven bowls came and talked with me, saying to me,* **"Come, I will show you the judgment of the great harlot who sits on many waters,** *2 "with whom the kings of the earth committed fornication, and the inhabitants of the earth were made drunk with the wine of her fornication." 3 So he carried me away in the Spirit into the wilderness. And* **I saw a woman sitting on a scarlet beast which was full of names of blasphemy, having seven heads and ten horns.** *4 The woman was arrayed in purple and scarlet, and adorned with gold and precious stones and pearls, having in her hand a golden cup full of abominations and the filthiness of her fornication. 5* **And on her forehead a name was written: MYSTERY, BABYLON THE GREAT, THE MOTHER OF HARLOTS AND OF THE ABOMINATIONS OF THE EARTH. 6 I saw the woman, drunk with the blood of the saints and with the blood of the martyrs of Jesus.** *And when I saw her, I marveled with great amazement.*

The woman represents the harlot church; she rides the beast system with seven heads and ten horns, pointing back to the beast in Daniel chapter 7 and the Dragon and the beast with ten horns in Revelations 12 and 13. The Harlot, the evil religious system, will prostitute their influence and sell her followers to the Antichrist in exchange for her personal safety, power, and wealth.

> ***Nahum 3:3*** *Horsemen charge with bright sword and glittering spear.* ***There is a multitude of slain, a great number of bodies, countless corpses-They stumble over the corpses 4 Because of the multitude of harlotries of the seductive harlot, the mistress of sorceries, who sells nations through her harlotries, And families through her sorceries.***

She gets used by the Antichrist to bring the religious sheep into Satan's flock. For much of history, the Popes controlled countries and kingdoms from the Vatican, and those days may return with a vengeance. The Harlot church will enforce the agendas of the Antichrist, paganism, and global fascism, and the religion of the new world order will force worship of the Antichrist and Satan. Worship will be mandatory for all, and the non-compliant dissenters and heretics will have their heads chopped off.

> ***Revelation 13*** *:13 He [the false prophet] performs great signs, so that he even makes fire come down from heaven on the earth in the sight of men. 14 And he deceives those who dwell on the earth by those signs which he was granted to do in the sight of the beast,* ***telling those who dwell on the earth to make an image to the beast who was wounded by the sword and lived. 15 He was granted power to give breath to the image of the beast, that the image of the beast should both speak and cause as many as would not worship the image of the beast to be killed.***

> ***Revelation 20:4*** *And I saw thrones, and they sat on them, and judgment was committed to them.* ***Then I saw the souls of those who had been beheaded for their witness to Jesus and for the word of God, who had not worshiped the beast or his image, and had not received his mark on their foreheads or on their hands.*** *And they lived and*

> *reigned with Christ for a thousand years.*

One clue as to the identity of the harlot is that she is a city sitting on seven hills. In Daniel's metallic man, the Roman Empire had two legs of iron, and the Roman Empire was divided into East and West. The capital of the west was Rome, and the capital of the east was Constantinople (now Istanbul), and both cities sit on seven hills. Many prophecy teachers believe the religious center for the global beast system, will be the Vatican in Rome.

> ***Revelation** 17:9 "Here is the mind which has wisdom: **The seven heads are seven mountains on which the woman sits.**
>
> **Revelation** 17:18 "And **the woman whom you saw is that great city which reigns over the kings of the earth."***

Ultimately, all who worship at the altar of the antichrist in the harlot church go to hell. Anyone who takes the mark of the beast is automatically beyond redemption; they have sold their souls to the Devil and are hell-bound after death.

> ***Revelation 14:9** Then a third angel followed them, saying with a loud voice,* **"If anyone worships the beast and his image, and receives his mark on his forehead or on his hand, 10 "he himself shall also drink of the wine of the wrath of God, which is poured out full strength into the cup of His indignation. He shall be tormented with fire and brimstone** *in the presence of the holy angels and in the presence of the Lamb. 11* **"And the smoke of their torment ascends forever and ever; and they have no rest day or night, who worship the beast and his image, and whoever receives the mark of his name."**
>
> ***Revelation 16:1** Then I heard a loud voice from the temple saying to the seven angels,* **"Go and pour out**

the bowls of the wrath of God on the earth." 2 So the first went and poured out his bowl upon the earth, and a foul and loathsome sore came upon the men who had the mark of the beast and those who worshiped his image.

2nd Leg - Global Finance

The beast system will control all resources and the ability to buy or sell anything; there will be a global finance system, and bartering or trading goods and services outside the system will be illegal and punished by death. The current globalists proclaim that everyone but the elite ruling class will "own nothing and be happy." One way they will accomplish their goal of owning all the food, land, and natural resources is by weaponizing the food supply.

The beast system will implement a strategy to make the world's population utterly dependent on the government for food, shelter, and their existence. We can see many examples of how food became weaponized in manufactured famines throughout history. The Communist Russians under Stalin and the Chinese under Mao starved tens of millions to gain power and enslave their nations.

One of the end-time signs is famines, which are among the judgments during the tribulation period. Cruelly, the beast system will initiate these food shortages and mass starvation to gain control over the earth's population. We see evidence of this already with the laws, restraints, and prohibitions placed on farmers to destroy the food supply in the name of climate change. The globalists have openly said they want to do away with beef, pork, and chicken and force the world to eat bugs and lab-grown meat. Globalist politicians, corporations, and elites are making aggressive moves for total control over all food, water, gas, coal, electrical energy, and every aspect of human life. That was precisely the purpose of the Covid shutdowns; it was a power grab and a global birth pain of the coming beast system.

We have a Biblical example that shows us how this works. Thanks to Joseph, Pharoah controlled the food supply during a **seven-year famine** (a type of the tribulation). The Pharoah weaponized the food supply to gain ownership over all the lands, crops, seeds, and cattle, and the people sold themselves into slavery for food.

> ***Genesis 47:13** Now **there was no bread in all the land; for the famine was very severe**, so that the land of Egypt and the land of Canaan languished because of the famine. 14 And **Joseph gathered up all the money that was found in the land** of Egypt and in the land of Canaan, for the grain which they bought; and Joseph brought the money into Pharoah's house. 15 **So when the money failed in the land** of Egypt and in the land of Canaan, all the Egyptians came to Joseph and said, "Give us bread, for why should we die in your presence? For the money has failed." 16 Then Joseph said, "Give your livestock, and I will give you bread for your livestock, if the money is gone." 17 So they brought their livestock to Joseph, and Joseph gave them bread in exchange for the horses, the flocks, the cattle of the herds, and for the donkeys. **Thus, he fed them with bread in exchange for all their livestock that year.** 18 When that year had ended, they came to him the next year and said to him, "We will not hide from my lord that our money is gone; my lord also has our herds of livestock. There is nothing left in the sight of my lord but our bodies and our lands. 19 "Why should we die before your eyes, both we and our land? Buy us and our land for bread, and we and our land will be servants of Pharaoh**; give us seed, that we may live and not die, that the land may not be desolate." 20 Then **Joseph bought all the land of Egypt for Pharaoh; for every man of the Egyptians sold his field, because the famine was severe upon them. So, the land became Pharaoh's.***

The Antichrist will control the planet by weaponizing the financial system and the ability to function or live in society. There will be no paper money; artificial intelligence will monitor all transactions using programmable digital currency and algorithms based on a social scoring system. Low social scores will limit, or ban access to bank accounts, and high social scores will gain privileges. Anyone who refuses to worship or identify with the Antichrist by taking his mark will get denied access to credit, bank accounts, and any possible way to buy or sell in the financial system.

> **Revelation 13:16 He causes ALL, both small and great, rich and poor, free and slave, to receive a mark on their right hand or on their foreheads, 17 and that no one may buy or sell except one who has the mark or the name of the beast, or the number of his name.** 18 Here is wisdom. Let him who has understanding calculate the number of the beast, for it is the number of a man: **His number is six hundred and sixty-six [666].**

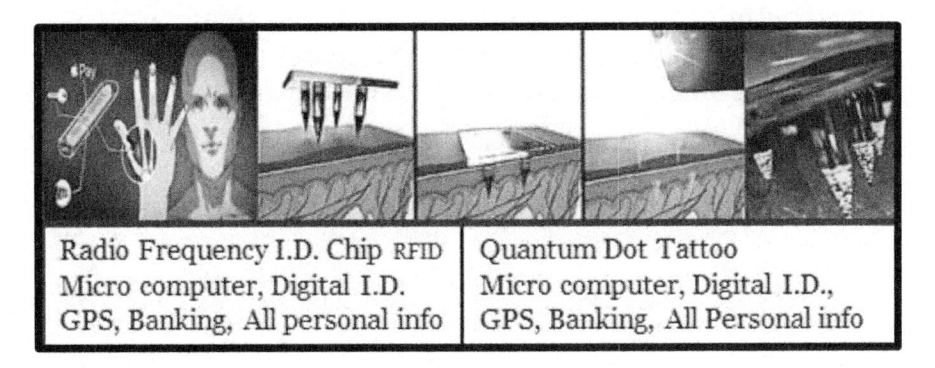

Radio Frequency I.D. Chip RFID Micro computer, Digital I.D. GPS, Banking, All personal info	Quantum Dot Tattoo Micro computer, Digital I.D., GPS, Banking, All Personal info

In the great tribulation, people will literally sell their souls for food. Paper money, gold, and silver will be useless in the beast system; if you can't eat it, then people will throw it in the streets. No amount of silver and gold can save anyone in the Day of the Lord. After World War 1 in Germany, in the Weimar Republic, in 1922, a loaf of bread cost 160 marks, but due to hyperinflation, in 1923, a loaf of bread cost 200,000,000,000. We can see why they would throw their money in the street.

***Ezekiel 7:19** 'They will throw their silver into the streets, and their gold will be like refuse; Their silver and their gold will not be able to deliver them in the day of the wrath of the LORD;* They will not satisfy their souls, **nor fill their stomachs**, because it became their stumbling block of iniquity.*

The beast financial system will be global fascism, which the current propaganda softens words like tyranny with phrases like public-private partnerships or stakeholder's interest instead of government control or blackmail. Big business will be in bed with the government; there will be no small businesses or middle class. There will only be two classes of people: the few in the elite ruling class and the rest with the low-class workers, virtual slaves. The useless eaters, those unable to work, disabled, old, or politically incorrect, will be killed first, like in Nazi Germany. The ruling class, big business oligarchs, will become extremely wealthy.

> ***Revelation 18:3*** *"For all the nations have drunk of the wine of the wrath of her fornication, the kings of the earth have committed fornication with her, **and the merchants of the earth have become rich through the abundance of her luxury.**"*

Because of hyperinflation, the servant class wages will not support a family. There will be famines and high prices so that a day's labor will only earn enough to buy one loaf of bread for the working man. But the elites will not suffer, enjoying good things like oil and wine.

> ***Revelation 6:6*** *And I heard a voice in the midst of the four living creatures saying,* **"A quart of wheat for a denarius, and three quarts of barley for a denarius [a day's wage]; and do not harm the oil and the wine."**

The merchants will be complicit in robbing the world's wealth. Look at the list of luxury items the elites will buy from the merchants and notice what is at the end of the list. They will sell the bodies and souls of men and children. There will be an open slave trade; it's happening now but in private. There was the case of Jeffrey Epstein enslaving children for the entertainment of pedophile politicians and elites, and unfortunately, it will only get far worse.

> ***Revelation 18::11*** *"And* **the merchants of the earth** *will weep and mourn over her, for no one buys their merchandise anymore: 12* **"merchandise of gold and silver, precious stones and pearls, fine linen and purple, silk and scarlet, every kind of citron wood, every kind of object of ivory, every kind of object of most precious wood, bronze, iron, and marble; 13 "and cinnamon and incense, fragrant oil and frankincense, wine and oil, fine flour and wheat, cattle and sheep, horses and chariots, and bodies and souls of men.**
>
> ***Joel 3:3*** **They have cast lots for My people, have given a boy as payment for a harlot, and sold a girl for wine, that they may drink.**

The merchants helped the harlot church and the Antichrist to deceive the world through sorcery. The word merchant does not refer to a small retail business but a wholesale provider or a big international corporation. **The Greek word for sorcery is pharmakeia, the root word for pharmacy or drugs**. Using or abusing drugs is like sorcery and can have a demonic spiritual impact on a person's life. How many lives have been destroyed by addiction to drugs? So, this verse implies that "big pharma" will help the government and fake religion to deceive the world through sorcery and drugs (vaccines).

Big Pharma unleashed untold damage, death, and loss of freedom with their Covid coup and the medical tyranny that followed. The shutdowns destroyed small businesses and churches. They doubled the wealth of the world's top ten wealthiest men by closing small businesses and sending their customers to international corporations. Politicians unlawfully seized emergency powers, with unparalleled authoritarianism and human rights violations worldwide. They mandated forced injections with an unproven experimental gene modification solution under the threat of job loss, the ability to enter public buildings and travel, etc., and corporations would not let anyone buy or sell without a mask. The pandemic was an example of how the antichrist global government can seize control of the world in the future, whether by war, intentional famines, lab-produced pestilences, bioweapons, or other planned catastrophes. They will not let a good disaster go to waste, It's textbook: problem - reaction - solution = more government control.

> **Revelation 18:23** *"The light of a lamp shall not shine in you anymore, and the voice of bridegroom and bride shall not be heard in you anymore.* ***For your merchants were the great men of the earth, for by your sorcery** [pharmakeia, pharmacy, drugs] **all the nations were deceived.***

3rd Leg - Rise of Antichrist

Only the Apostle John uses the name antichrist, but he has many names in the Bible. The word Antichrist does not mean the opposite of Christ. **In Greek, anti can mean opposed to, or instead of, so we can combine the two to say, one who imitates Christ to oppose Christ.**

Jesus Christ	Antichrist
Holy Trinity, Father, Son, Holy Spirit	Evil Trinity Satan, antichrist, false prophet
God incarnate	Satan incarnate
Makes a new covenant with all who believe and gives eternal salvation	Confirms a covenant with Israel and breaks it in 3 1/2 years
Entered Most Holy in Heaven to atone for the sin of the world	Enters Most Holy in Jewish temple commits an abomination
Miracles by the Spirit of God	Miracles by Satanic power
Resurrected from the Dead	Resurrects from head wound
King of kings and Lord of lords	Global dictator, over 10 kings
Preached in hell before ascending to highest heaven, rules over all	Ascends from pit to rule earth, Satan gives him power 3 1/2 years
Bridegroom to the Church, Bride of Christ a chaste virgin to Christ	Fornicates with whore of Babylon, Religious Harlot, idolatry, sorcery
Preceded by John the Baptist	Promoted by the false prophet
Jesus earthly ministry 3 1/2 years His blood forgives, saves, heals	Kills saints 3 1/2 years, he is drunk with blood of saints, power
Represented as coming on a white horse with sword/army behind him	Represented as coming on a white horse, with a bow, no arrows
Who can make war with the Lamb? Christ destroys world's armies, judges the world, cast antichrist into lake of fire, imprisons Satan	Who can make war with the beast? He kills saints, lays siege to Jerusalem, Christ appears and cast antichrist into Lake of Fire

This political leader will come looking like he is the one who can save the world. Christians are looking for Christ to return, Jews are looking for their Messiah, Muslims are looking for the Madhi, and Buddhists are looking for the Maitreya; the Antichrist will come on the world scene and portray himself as the one they were waiting for. With a small following, the Antichrist will rise from obscurity to ascend to the pinnacle of power because of his Satanic authority, demonic influence, cunning schemes, manipulation, and deceit. He will be a charismatic leader who will negotiate, intimidate, uproot, and remove his political opponents on the road to becoming a tyrannical global dictator.

> **Daniel 11:21** "And in his place shall arise **a vile person, to whom they will not give the honor of royalty; but he shall come in peaceably, and seize the kingdom by intrigue.** 22 "With the force of a flood they shall be swept away from before him and be broken, and also the prince of the covenant. 23 **"And after the league is made with him he shall act deceitfully, for he shall come up and become strong with a small number of people.**
>
> **Daniel 8:23** "At the latter period of their reign, When the transgressors have finished, **A king will arise insolent and skilled in intrigue and cunning.".** Amplified Version
>
> **Daniel 8:23** "And in the **latter time** of their kingdom, when the **transgressors have reached their fullness**, **A king shall arise, having fierce features, who understands sinister schemes.** 24 **His power shall be mighty, but not by his own power; He shall destroy fearfully**, and shall prosper and thrive; He shall destroy the mighty, and also the holy people. 25 **"Through his cunning He shall cause deceit to prosper under his rule; And he shall exalt himself in his heart. He shall destroy many in their prosperity.** He shall even rise against the Prince of princes; But he shall be broken without human means.

The Restrainer

An angel instructed Daniel that the words, or specific details, about his vision would be closed up and sealed until the time of the end. One hundred years ago, people could not imagine how anyone could control the global population so that nobody could buy or sell without the mark of the beast. Even fifty years ago, that wasn't possible, but the technology is here, and some countries like China are forcing that technology on their people. It's only a matter of time before things are ready for the beast system and the Antichrist to arrive.

> ***Daniel 12:9** And he said, "Go your way, Daniel, **for the words are closed up and sealed till the time of the end.***

Even though the time is approaching, guessing the identity of the Antichrist is not wise. Everyone who has declared who the Antichrist is has been proven false. The set time for the Antichrist to appear on the world stage comes after the rapture when the restrainer gets removed. Then, the Antichrist can come forward and confirm a covenant with Israel.

Most Bible teachers agree that the Holy Spirit in the church or individual believers makes a restraining force that prevents and suppresses evil in the world. The Antichrist cannot come forward until after the Spirit-filled church gets taken up in the rapture.

> ***2 Thessalonians 2:3** Let no one deceive you by any means; for **that Day will not come unless the falling away comes first, and the man of sin is revealed, the son of perdition [antichrist], ... 6 And now you know what is restraining, that he may be revealed in his own time. 7 For the mystery of lawlessness is already at work; only He who now restrains will do so until He is taken out of the way.***

We should point out that "the restrainer" is God. God has restrained himself since the first sin in the Garden of Eden. God should have destroyed Adam and Eve but restrained himself because of his mercy, compassion, and forgiveness. Every human is a sinner and deserves God's judgment; if not for God's mercy, we would all be destroyed. And thank God, his mercies are new every morning.

> ***Lamentations 3:19** Remembering mine affliction and my misery, the wormwood and the gall. 20 My soul hath them still in remembrance, and is humbled in me. 21 This I recall to my mind, therefore have I hope. 22 **It is of the LORD'S mercies that we are not consumed, because his compassions fail not. 23 They are new every morning: great is thy faithfulness.***

God is the restrainer; he controls the universe, and if he did not restrain the Devil, Satan would destroy every person on earth. We know God protected Job, and Satan had to get permission to attack him. But God set boundaries of what Satan could do when he attacked Job.

> ***Job 1:8** Then the LORD said to Satan, "Have you considered My servant Job, that there is none like him on the earth, a blameless and upright man, one who fears God and shuns evil?" 9 **So Satan answered the LORD and said, "Does Job fear God for nothing? 10 "Have You not made a hedge around him, around his household, and around all that he has on every side?** You have blessed the work of his hands, and his possessions have increased in the land. 11 "But now, stretch out Your hand and touch all that he has, and he will surely curse You to Your face!" 12 And the LORD said to Satan, **"Behold, all that he has is in your power; only do not lay a hand on his person."** So, Satan went out from the presence of the LORD.*

The restrainer will be active after the rapture during the tribulation. God has reserved judgments to release in the tribulation period, namely seven seals, trumpets, and bowls of wrath and judgment, which God holds back until his time to release them. The book of Revelation clearly shows how God seals people and restrains the destroyers until their appointed time to come forward, keeping them from touching the sealed saints while destruction happens to the sinners around them.

Revelation 7:1 *After these things I saw four angels standing at the four corners of the earth, holding the four winds of the earth, that the wind should not blow on the earth, on the sea, or on any tree. 2* ***Then I saw another angel ascending from the east, having the seal of the living God. And he cried with a loud voice to the four angels to whom it was granted to harm the earth and the sea, 3 saying, "Do not harm the earth, the sea, or the trees till we have sealed the servants of our God on their foreheads."***

Revelation 9:1 *Then the fifth angel sounded: And I saw a star fallen from heaven to the earth. To him was given the key to the bottomless pit. 2* ***And he opened the bottomless pit,*** *and smoke arose out of the pit like the smoke of a great furnace. So, the sun and the air were darkened because of the smoke of the pit. 3 Then out of the smoke locusts came upon the earth. And to them was given power, as the scorpions of the earth have power.* ***4 They were commanded not to harm the grass of the earth, or any green thing, or any tree, but only those men who do not have the seal of God on their foreheads.***

Revelation 9:13 *Then the sixth angel sounded: And I heard a voice from the four horns of the golden altar which is before God, 14 saying to the sixth angel who had the trumpet,* ***"Release the four angels who are bound at the great river Euphrates." 15 So the four angels, who had been prepared for the hour and day and month and year, were released to kill a third of mankind.***

The fact that God distinguishes between believers and unbelievers affirms that God has not appointed the church to wrath. However, God sometimes allows judgment as a chastisement to bring people to repentance and salvation. There will be multitudes who die as martyrs in the tribulation.

What their spiritual condition was before the rapture, we don't know. Possibly, they enter the tribulation period as unbelievers or professing believers who have backslidden, living in sin, and were separated from God. The suffering and peril they encounter may turn them to Christ in repentance and salvation before dying for their faith. All the Jews who endure until the end of the tribulation will become believers in Jesus and get saved. God is a God of mercy and forgiveness and desires all men to get saved. But man has free will to choose, and those who refuse to repent in the tribulation will experience the wrath of God.

Daniel's 70th week

God's purpose for the tribulation is to save the Jews and judge the world. Israel begins the tribulation as unbelievers in Christ, but all Israel that survive the great tribulation will turn to Christ and get saved. God gave Daniel a prophetic time frame of 70 weeks, each week being seven years, foretelling the exact day, Palm Sunday, that Jesus would enter Jerusalem for the Passover at the end of the 69th week. That prophetic timetable is in Daniel 9:24, 25 & 26 (A). Daniel 9:26 (B) gives the prophecies about the 70th week and how it begins with a covenant between the Antichrist and the nation of Israel, which will be the official start of the tribulation period.

> ***Daniel 9:24** `Seventy weeks are determined for thy people, and for thy holy city, to shut up the transgression, and to seal up sins, and to cover iniquity, and to bring in righteousness age-during, and to seal up vision and prophet, and to anoint the holy of holies. "Know therefore and understand, that from the going forth of the command to restore and build Jerusalem Until Messiah the Prince,* **there shall be seven weeks and sixty-two weeks (7+62=69 weeks); The street shall be built again, and the wall, even in troublesome times.** *26 (A) "And after the sixty-wo weeks Messiah shall be cut off, but not for Himself; (1st coming)*

Daniel's 70 Weeks

In Daniel's prophecy of 70 weeks, he prophesied to the exact day that Messiah (Jesus) would enter Jerusalem on Palm Sunday 483 years in the future. Daniel's prophecy said from the command to rebuild the second temple to the Messiah will be 69 weeks of 7 years or 483 years. The command to rebuild the temple came on March 14, 445 B.C., to get the correct date of the appearance of Messiah we have to convert the Jewish 360-day calendar to the Roman 365-day calendar and account for the leap years differences, according and Jewish practices. 483 years x 360 days = 173,880 days converted to the Roman calendar is 476 years & 24 days.

> **Daniel 9:24-26** "*Seventy weeks are determined for your people and for your holy city, to finish the transgression,* To *make an end of sins, To make reconciliation for iniquity, To bring in everlasting righteousness, To seal up vision and prophecy, and to anoint the Most Holy.* "*Know therefore and understand, that from the going forth of the command to restore and build Jerusalem until Messiah the Prince, there shall be seven weeks and sixty-two weeks; The street shall be built again, and the wall, even in troublesome times.* "*And after the sixty-two weeks Messiah shall be cut off,* but not for Himself;

173,740 days	173,740 days = 476 years
24 days	March 14 counting forward 24 days
116 days	116 days added for leap years
173,880 days	**483 years or 69 weeks of 7 years**

The prophet Zechariah also prophesied about Jesus' entry into Jerusalem on a donkey, over 550 years before Christ entered Jerusalem on Palm Sunday.

Jesus completed the first 69 weeks of the prophecy when he entered and wept over Jerusalem for the Passover and crucifixion.

> *Luke 19:41* *Now as He drew near, He saw the city and wept over it, 42 saying,* **"If you had known, even you, especially in this your day, the things that make for your peace! But now they are hidden from your eyes.**
>
> *Matthew 23:37* *"O Jerusalem, Jerusalem, the one who kills the prophets and stones those who are sent to her! How often I wanted to gather your children together, as a hen gathers her chicks under her wings, but you were not willing! 38 "See! Your house is left to you desolate; 39* **"for I say to you, you shall see Me no more till you say, 'Blessed is He who comes in the name of the LORD!'"**

Regardless of what anyone may say, the tribulation begins when a covenant between Israel and the Antichrist is confirmed. All the end times signs lead up to that point. That covenant is the 70th week of Daniel's vision; the symbolism of a week in the passage is a week of years or seven years.

> *Daniel 9:26 (B) And the people of* **the prince who is to come Shall destroy the city and the sanctuary. The end of it shall be with a flood,** *and till the end of the war desolations are determined.* *27* Then **he shall confirm a covenant with many for one week [7 years].**

Once the covenant is confirmed, the tribulation begins, and the countdown clock starts ticking: 3 1/2 years to the abomination of desolation and seven years until the second coming of Christ.

Tribulation begins

We get the first look at the Antichrist in the book of Revelation when the Lamb, Jesus, opens the first of seven seals. Jesus opens the seal so he is not the rider on the white horse releasing himself; the rider on the first horse is the Antichrist.

The rider comes into power with military intimidation, threatening with a bow but no arrows. Antichrist's crown or power and authority are given to him by Satan. He goes forth to conquer, meaning he has not conquered or shot any arrows yet. He will start with a false peace and look like the world's savior, but he is the false Christ and becomes progressively more violent until at least 58% of the world's population, and likely much more, dies during the seven years of his reign. There are about 8 billion people in the world, so with today's numbers, 58% fatalities from just the 4th seal and the 6th trumpet would be 4.6 billion people. We have no clue how many will die from the other judgments, plagues, martyrdoms, and the battle of Armageddon at the second coming.

> *Revelation 6:1 Now I saw when **the Lamb opened one of the seals**; and I heard one of the four living creatures saying with a voice like thunder, "Come and see." 2 And I looked, and **behold, a white horse. He who sat on it had a bow; and a crown was given to him, and he went out conquering and to conquer.***

> *Daniel 11:21 "And in his place shall arise **a vile person, to whom they will not give the honor of royalty; but he shall come in peaceably, and***

> *seize the kingdom by intrigue.* 22 *"With the force of a flood they shall be swept away from before him and be broken, and also the prince of the covenant.* 23 ***"And after the league is made with him he shall act deceitfully,*** *for he shall come up and become strong with a small number of people.*
>
> *1 Thessalonians 5:2 For you yourselves know perfectly that **the day of the Lord** so comes as a thief in the night. 3 For **when they say, "Peace and safety!" then sudden destruction comes upon them**, as labor pains upon a pregnant woman. **And they shall not escape.***

The white horse represents the beast system, the fascist government that the Antichrist will rule. Just as the rider on the white horse personifies the son of Satan coming to bring hell on earth, the following three horses also have riders; those horses represent war, famine, and death; their riders represent man's cruelty to man. We cannot estimate how much of the torment, suffering, and death during the tribulation directly results from the deliberate actions of demon-possessed men.

Power struggles

Daniel gives many details about the Antichrist, calling his global government the fourth beast, and the Antichrist is called the little horn, and he will be the last Gentile dictator to dominate the world. Antichrist obtains power by defeating three other kings with shrewd dealings, tactics, and military battles.

> ***Daniel 7:19*** *"Then I wished to know the truth about the fourth beast, which was different from all the others, **exceedingly dreadful, with its teeth of iron and its nails of bronze, which devoured, broke in pieces, and trampled the residue with its feet;** 20 **"and the ten horns that were on its head, and the other horn which came up, before which three fell, namely, that horn** which had eyes and a*

mouth which spoke pompous words, whose appearance was greater than his fellows.

Daniel 7:23 The fourth beast shall be a fourth kingdom *on earth, which shall be different from all other kingdoms,* **and shall devour the whole earth, trample it and break it in pieces. 24 The ten horns are ten kings who shall arise from this kingdom. And another shall rise after them; He shall be different from the first ones, and shall subdue three kings.**

Besides fighting to suppress the power struggles and conflicts within his kingdom, the Antichrist would go to war with the Two Witnesses. These two Jewish prophets will operate with the power of God to call down fire from heaven and call for plagues and droughts against their enemies in the beast system. But the witnesses are only given this power for the first 3 1/2 years; when they complete their mission, they get killed by the Antichrist. However, the Antichrist is stricken with a mortal head wound and ascends out of the bottomless pit of Hell to kill them. After that, the Antichrist is given power for 3 ½ years to kill the saints.

Revelation 11:3 *"And* **I will give power to my two witnesses, and they will prophesy one thousand two hundred and sixty days [3 ½ years]***, clothed in sackcloth." ... 5 And if anyone wants to harm them, fire proceeds from their mouth and devours their enemies. And if anyone wants to harm them, he must be killed in this manner. 6 These have power to shut heaven, so that no rain falls in the days of their prophecy; and they have power over waters to turn them to blood, and to strike the earth with all plagues, as often as they desire. 7* **When they finish their testimony, the beast that ascends out of the bottomless pit will make war against them, overcome them, and kill them.***"*

Apparently, in the battles with the three kings *(3 horns)*, and the two witnesses, at some point in time, the Antichrist suffers a mortal head wound from a weapon *(sword)*, at which point his right eye is put out, and his arm gets destroyed.

> ***Zechariah 11:15*** *And the LORD said to me, "Next, take for yourself the implements of **a foolish shepherd**. 16 "For indeed I will raise up a shepherd in the land who will not care for those who are cut off, nor seek the young, nor heal those that are broken, nor feed those that still stand. **But he will eat the flesh of the fat and tear their hooves in pieces. 17 "Woe to the worthless shepherd, who leaves the flock! A sword shall be against his arm and against his right eye; His arm shall completely wither, and his right eye shall be totally blinded.***"

Some say this death was political, others that it was physical. Two points imply that it is physical; first, that he ascends from the pit of hell. The second point is related to the first: he will claim to be the resurrected from the dead, imitating Christ. They will say that the Antichrist "was *(alive)* and is not *(he died)*, and yet is *(he resurrected)*."

> ***Revelation 17:8*** *"**The beast that you saw was, and is not, and will ascend out of the bottomless pit and go to perdition.** And those who dwell on the earth will marvel, whose names are not written in the Book of Life from the foundation of the world, **when they see the beast that was, and is not, and yet is.***
>
> ***Revelation 13:3*** *And **I saw one of his heads as if it had been mortally wounded, and his deadly wound was healed.***

> *A sword shall be against his arm and against his right eye; His arm shall completely wither, and his right eye shall be totally blinded."* Zechariah 11:17

The all-seeing eye is a pagan symbol going back to ancient Egypt, is used as a logo by Free Masons, and is on the US dollar bill. A single eye can also represent the Antichrist, and many modern celebrities and artists embrace that spirit when they cover one eye in their photos.

After seeing the Antichrist defeat the three kings and the two witnesses and then revive after a mortal head wound, fear will come over the earth, and people will say, who can make war with him? When Antichrist rises from the pit, Satan will possess him, and he will become a beast and he will go into a demonic murderous rage unlike anything seen on earth.

> *And all the world marveled and followed the beast. 4 So they worshiped the dragon who gave authority to the beast; and they worshiped the beast, saying, "Who is like the beast? Who is able to make war with him?"*

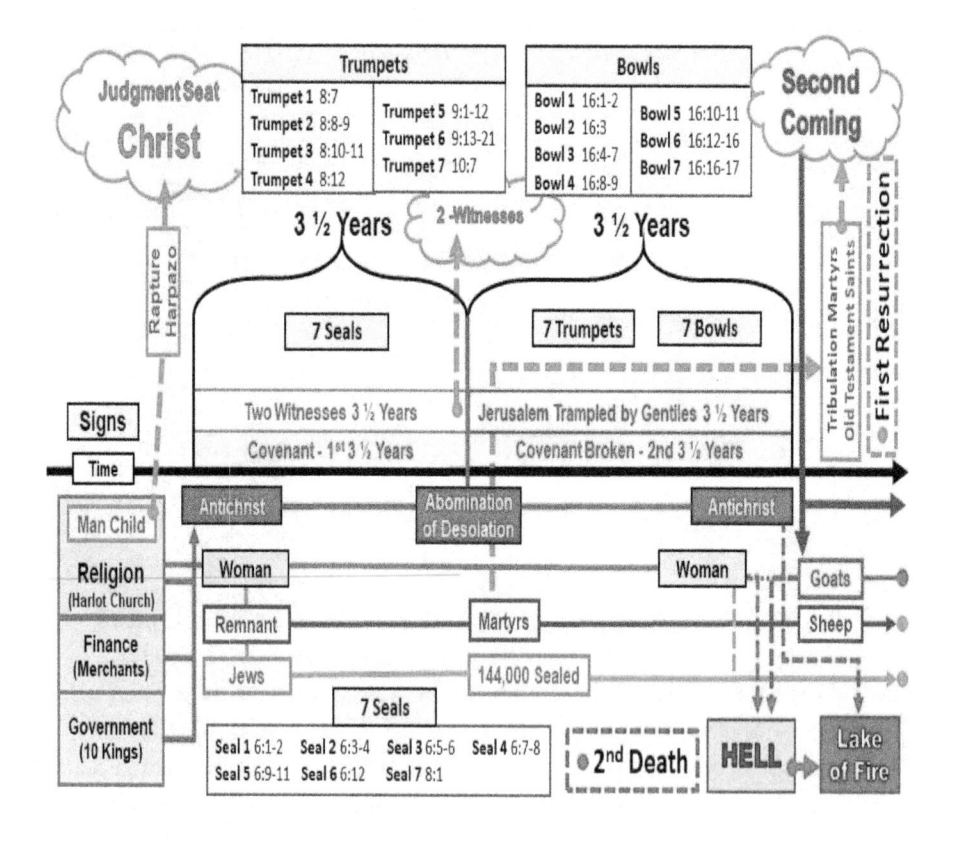

Mid-Trib turning point

In the middle of the seven years, at the 3 1/2-year mark, Satan will anoint his man, the Antichrist. The seven heads and ten horns we saw on the Dragon, Satan, in Revelation 12, along with his power, throne, and authority, are given to the Antichrist. From that time, all hell will break loose on the earth, and it will be the worst time of suffering in the history of the world.

> ***Revelation 13:1*** *Then I stood on the sand of the sea. And I saw a beast rising up out of the sea, **having seven heads and ten horns, and on his horns ten crowns**, and on his heads a blasphemous name. 2 Now the beast which I saw was like a **leopard**, his feet were like the feet of a **bear**, and his mouth like the mouth of a **lion. The dragon gave him his power, his throne, and great authority**.*

Then God puts it into the hearts of the ten kings to give all their power and authority to the Antichrist so he has no opposition. But that power is for a very short time.

> ***Revelation 17:12** "The **ten horns** which you saw are **ten kings** who have received no kingdom as yet, **but they receive authority for one hour as kings with the beast. 13** "These are of one mind, and they will give their power and authority to the beast.*
>
> ***Revelation 17:17** "For God has put it into their hearts to fulfill His purpose, to be of one mind, and to give their kingdom to the beast, until the words of God are fulfilled.*

In another imitation of Christ, the Antichrist Satanic reign of power will last for 3 1/2 years, about the same amount of time as Jesus' earthly ministry, but with the opposite results. Antichrist starts by cursing God and the heavenly host of angels, declaring himself a god, and forcing everyone to worship him.

> ***Revelation 13:5** And he was given a mouth **speaking great things and blasphemies, and he was given authority to continue for forty-two months [3 ½ years].** 6 Then he opened his mouth in **blasphemy** against God, to blaspheme His name, His tabernacle, and those who dwell in heaven. 7 **It was granted to him to make war with the saints and to overcome them. And authority was given him over every tribe, tongue, and nation. 8 All who dwell on the earth will worship him**, whose names have not been written in the Book of Life of the Lamb slain from the foundation of the world.*

In the middle of the seven-year covenant, the Antichrist will enter the temple of God in Jerusalem and defile it, setting up an image of himself as a god. Then, the secular Israeli politicians, rulers, and leaders who negotiated the covenant with the

Antichrist, thinking they would be exempt from persecution, will be the first to get destroyed. After the Antichrist commits the abominations in the temple, there will be an overflowing scourge of death that begins at the temple, becomes a flood, and spreads, and the Gentiles will trample Jerusalem.

> ***Isaiah 28:14*** *Therefore hear the word of the LORD, you scornful men, who rule this people who are in Jerusalem, 15* **Because you have said, "We have made a covenant with death, And with Sheol [Hell] we are in agreement. When the overflowing scourge passes through, it will not come to us, for we have made lies our refuge, and under falsehood we have hidden ourselves."** *... 17 Also I will make justice the measuring line, and righteousness the plummet;* **The hail will sweep away the refuge of lies, And the waters will overflow the hiding place. 18 Your covenant with death will be annulled, and your agreement with Sheol [Hell] will not stand; When the overflowing scourge passes through, then you will be trampled down by it.**
>
> ***Daniel 11:21*** *"And in his place shall arise* **a vile person***, to whom they will not give the honor of royalty; but* **he shall come in peaceably, and seize the kingdom by intrigue. 22 "With the force of a flood they shall be swept away from before him and be broken, and also the prince of the covenant. 23 "And after the league is made with him, he shall act deceitfully,** *for he shall come up and become strong with a small number of people.*

This scourge will end with the death of two-thirds of the global Jewish population, a fate far worse than the Holocaust.

> ***Zechariah 13:8*** *And it shall come to pass in all the land," Says the LORD,* **"That two-thirds in it shall be cut off and die, but one -third shall be left in**

*it: 9 **I will bring the one-third through the fire**, Will refine them as silver is refined, and test them as gold is tested. **They will call on My name, And I will answer them.** I will say, 'This is My people'; And each ne will say, 'The LORD is my God.'"*

Abomination of Desolation – Jerusalem, Temple
Antichrist, False Prophet, Image of the Beast

Abomination of desolation

The breaking of the covenant is a focal point in Bible prophecy; even Jesus made reference to it. Jesus called it the abomination of desolation, which happens when the Antichrist enters the temple in Jerusalem, sets up an image of himself, and declares that he is a god. Of course, this implies that the Jewish people will rebuild the temple and that animal sacrifices will be re-instituted, which could happen any time before the middle of the tribulation.

> ***Matthew 24:15-16*** *"Therefore **when you see the 'abomination of desolation,' spoken of by Daniel the prophet, standing in the holy place"** (whoever reads, let him understand), **"then let those who are in Judea flee to the mountains.***

***2 Thessalonians 2:3 Let no one deceive you** by any means; for that Day will not come unless **the falling away comes first, and the man of sin** [antichrist] **is revealed, the son of perdition, who opposes and exalts himself above all that is called God or that is worshiped, so that he sits as God in the temple of God, showing himself that he is God.**

Ezekiel 8:5 Then He said to me, "Son of man, lift your eyes now toward the north." So, I lifted my eyes toward the north, and there, **north of the altar gate**, was this **image of jealousy** in the entrance. 6 Furthermore He said to me, "Son of man, **do you see what they are doing, the great abominations that the house of Israel commits here, to make Me go far away from My sanctuary? Now turn again, you will see greater abominations."**

Revelation 13:13-14 He [false prophet] **performs great signs, so that he even makes fire come down from heaven on the earth in the sight of men. And he deceives those who dwell on the earth by those signs** which he was granted to do in the sight of the beast, telling those who dwell on the earth **to make an image to the beast** who was wounded by the sword and lived. He was granted power to give breath to the image of the beast, that the image of the beast should both speak **and cause as many as would not worship the image of the beast to be killed.***

The following is Daniel's description of the abomination of desolations. Daniel says that the Antichrist will take away the daily sacrifice, which again implies that the temple gets rebuilt and the restoration of the Levitical priesthood, animal sacrifices, and offerings before the middle of the tribulation period.

Daniel 9:26 But in the middle of the week, He shall bring an end to sacrifice and offering. And on the wing of abominations shall be one who makes desolate, even until the consummation, which is determined, Is poured out on the desolate."

Daniel 11: 31 "And forces shall be mustered by him, and they shall defile the sanctuary fortress; then they shall take away the daily sacrifices, and place there the abomination of desolation. 32 "Those who do wickedly against the covenant he shall corrupt with flattery; but the people who know their God shall be strong, and carry out great exploits. 33 "And those of the people who understand shall instruct many; *yet for many days they shall fall by sword and flame, by captivity and plundering.*

*Daniel 8:9 And out of one of them came **a little horn*** which grew exceedingly great toward the south, toward the east, and toward the Glorious Land. 10 ***And it grew up to the host of heaven; and it cast down some of the host and some of the stars to the ground, and trampled them.*** 11 ***He even exalted himself as high as the Prince of the host; and by him the daily sacrifices were taken away, and the place of His sanctuary was cast down.*** 12 ***Because of transgression, an army was given over to the horn to oppose the daily sacrifices; and he cast truth down to the ground.*** He did all this and prospered.

First, the Antichrist commits abominations in the temple in Jerusalem. After that, the temple grounds get trampled, and armies surround and attack Jerusalem. There will be Jews who see the abominations and weep. God will put his mark on them, sealing and protecting them from harm and restraining the destroyers from touching them.

Ezekiel 9:2** And suddenly **six men came from the direction of the upper gate, which faces north, each with his battle-ax in his hand. One man among them was clothed with linen and had a writer's inkhorn at his side.** They went in and stood beside the bronze altar. 3 Now the glory of the God of Israel had gone up from the cherub, where it had been, to the threshold of the temple. And He called to the man clothed with linen, who had the writer's inkhorn at his side; 4 and the LORD said to him, **"Go through the midst of the city, through the midst of Jerusalem, and put a mark on the foreheads of the men who sigh and cry over all the abominations that are done within it." 5 To the others He said in my hearing, "Go after him through the city and kill; do not let your eye spare, nor have any pity. 6 "Utterly slay old and young men, maidens and little children and women; but do not come near anyone on whom is the mark; and begin at My sanctuary."** So, they began with the elders who were before the temple. 7 Then He said to them, **"Defile the temple, and fill the courts with the slain. Go out!" And they went out and killed in the city.

Mark of the Beast

After declaring himself a god, the Antichrist will seize control of everyone's money, and nobody can buy or sell anything without taking a mark of allegiance to him. Think of the whole world switching to a programmable digital currency that the central bank of the global government controls; access to funds, buying or selling is monitored and controlled by artificial intelligence through algorithms based on a social scoring system. Total submission to the dictates of the beast system will control every penny and, ultimately, life or death.

Access to money, goods, and services based on a social credit scoring system is already operational in China. If someone says or does anything the government doesn't like, they can get locked out of the system and lose life's privileges or essentials. The philosophy of that system is already gaining acceptance with globalist politicians and corporations worldwide. What happens when the government locks you out of your bank account, blocks credit cards, and denies travel and access to basic needs? The Covid shutdowns were a test run for the Antichrist's new world order, and they will never stop until they conquer and dominate the world completely.

> ***Revelation 13:16-18 He causes all, both small and great, rich and poor, free and slave, to receive a mark on their right hand or on their foreheads, 17 and that no one may buy or sell except one who has the mark or the name of the beast, or the number of his name.*** *Here is wisdom. Let him who has understanding calculate the number of the beast, for it is the number of a man: His number is six hundred and sixty-six [666].*

The False Prophet

The leader of all the world's religions will be the false prophet. He will bring the world's religions into the beast system and be the enforcer that makes them bow to worship the image of the Antichrist or face death. He will have Satanic powers, doing miracles, signs, and wonders to deceive the world. Many believe the prime candidate for this position is the Roman Catholic Pope since the Antichrist will rule from the territory of the old Roman Empire, and the Vatican could be the global religious center. Also, the Pope has 1.3 billion followers and tremendous wealth to use as bargaining chips to gain more power in the beast system.

> ***Revelation 13:13-14** He [false prophet] **performs great signs, so that he even makes fire come down from heaven on the earth in the sight of men. And he deceives those who dwell on the earth by those signs** which he was granted to do in the sight of the beast, telling those who dwell on the earth **to make an image to the beast** who was wounded by the sword and lived. He was granted power to give breath to the image of the beast, that the image of the beast should both speak **and cause as many as would not worship the image of the beast to be killed.***

We can use the German churches under Hitler as an example of how this could happen. Germany was the home of Martin Luther and the protestant reformation, and the majority of the country was professing Lutherans. In less than a year under Hitler they forsook Christ and became complicit in Hitler's atrocities and insanity. A worse dictator than Hitler is coming, and far worse pressures and horrors await those who refuse to bow to him. But those who take the mark of the beast and bow to his image have eternal torment waiting for them.

> ***Revelation 14:9** Then a third angel followed them, saying with a loud voice, **"If anyone worships the beast and his image, and receives his mark on his forehead or on his hand, "he himself shall also drink of the wine of the wrath of God, which is poured out full strength into the cup of His indignation. He shall be tormented with fire and brimstone in the presence of the holy angels and in the presence of the Lamb. "And the smoke of their torment ascends forever and ever; and they have no rest day or night, who worship the beast and his image, and whoever receives the mark of his name."***

Like Hitler's Germany, Stalin's Russia, Mao's China, and some religious sects like Islam, family members will report their fathers and mothers, brothers and sisters to the authorities to be imprisoned or put to death in zeal for the revolution, religion, or in fear to save their own lives. History will repeat itself. To a lesser extent, the same type of reactions happened with the COVID mask requirements, neighbors and random strangers attacking people in public for not wearing a mask. That shows that we can have the same reaction under the same circumstances. The atmosphere of persecution in the tribulation will be far greater than anything the world has ever seen with a vicious global tyranny in a digital surveillance concentration camp. There will be cameras everywhere, along with more innovative smartphones, which will eventually get replaced by chips implanted under the skin. Big Brother is the Antichrist, and he will track everyone with GPS and analyze every movement, interaction, and thought with artificial intelligence and algorithms.

> **Matthew 24:10** "And then **many will be offended, will betray one another, and will hate one another.**
>
> **Luke 21:12** "But before all these things, **they will lay their hands on you and persecute you**, delivering you up to the synagogues and prisons. You will be brought before kings and rulers for My name's sake.
>
> **Luke 21:16** "**You will be betrayed even by parents and brothers, relatives and friends; and they will put some of you to death.** 17 "And you will be hated by all for My name's sake.
>
> **Mark 13:12** "Now **brother will betray brother to death, and a father his child; and children will rise up against parents and cause them to be put to death. 13 "And you will be hated by all for My name's sake.** But he who endures to the end shall be saved.

In the picture, a Canadian Pastor got arrested for conducting church services during the COVID shutdown. Persecution against churches, pastors, and believers will eventually become deadly everywhere; it's just a question of when. It's already happening in many parts of the world.

How long oh Lord?

The final 3 ½ years of the tribulation called Jacob's Trouble *(Jeremiah 30:7)* will be worse than the holocaust: 2/3 of all Jews die, 1/4 of the world's population is killed at one time, followed by another 1/3 of the people getting killed at another time. At the beginning of the tribulation, John saw in his vision martyrs asking God, "How long, oh Lord," until the murderers get judged? And the response was until their fellow servants get killed. The suffering, death, and murders will not end until Jesus returns and destroys the final Gentile empire, the Antichrist government, making the "Times of the Gentiles" come to an end.

> ***Revelation 6:9** When **He opened the fifth seal, I saw under the altar the souls of those who had been slain for the word of God and for the testimony which they held**. 10 And they cried with a loud voice, saying, **"How long, O Lord, holy and true, until You judge and avenge our blood on those who dwell on the earth?"** 11 Then a white robe was given to each of them; and it was said to them that they should rest a little while longer, **until both the number of their fellow servants and their brethren, who would be killed as they were, was completed.***
>
> ***Revelation 11:1** Then I was given a reed like a measuring rod. And the angel stood, saying, "Rise and measure the temple of God, the altar, and those who*

*worship there. 2 **"But leave out the court which is outside the temple, and do not measure it, for it has been given to the Gentiles. And they will tread the holy city underfoot for forty-two months [3 ½ years].***

*Luke 21:22 "For **these are the days of vengeance**, that all things which are written may be fulfilled. 23 "But woe to those who are pregnant and to those who are nursing babies in those days! **For there will be great distress in the land and wrath upon this people. 24 "And they will fall by the edge of the sword, and be led away captive into all nations. And Jerusalem will be trampled by Gentiles until the times of the Gentiles are fulfilled.***

Persecutes the saints

The saints, believers present during the seven years of tribulation, will be targeted for death under this regime; in particular, during the last three and half years, the Antichrist is given authority to kill the saints.

*Daniel 7:23 25 He shall speak pompous words against the Most High**, shall persecute the saints of the Most High,** And shall intend to change times and law. **Then the saints shall be given into his hand for a time and times and half a time [3 ½ years].***

Daniel 7:23 21 "I was watching; and the same horn was making war against the saints, and prevailing against them,

Once the Antichrist is permitted to wage war with the saints, he will begin a murderous rampage and rule the world with an iron fist.

> **Revelation 13:3** *And I saw one of his heads as if it had been mortally wounded, and his deadly wound was healed.* **And all the world marveled and followed the beast.** *4* **So they worshiped the dragon who gave authority to the beast; and they worshiped the beast, saying, "Who is like the beast? Who is able to make war with him?"** *5 And he was given a mouth speaking great things and blasphemies,* **and he was given authority to continue for forty-two months [3 ½ years].** *6 Then he opened his mouth in blasphemy against God, to blaspheme His name, His tabernacle, and those who dwell in heaven. 7* **It was granted to him to make war with the saints and to overcome them. And authority was given him over every tribe, tongue, and nation.**

We can only imagine how religious leaders who volunteer to worship the Antichrist and take his mark will take pleasure in killing Christians who would be intensely loathed and hated for going against the system. Some of those religious leaders (Muslim, Hindu) would probably like to kill Christians now, how much more in the tribulation with whirlwinds of demonic activity swirling around them.

> **Revelation 17:6** *I saw the woman, drunk with the blood of the saints and with the blood of the martyrs of Jesus.* *And when I saw her, I marveled with great amazement.*

God, in his mercy, will reach out to the people being led astray by the false prophet and the Antichrist and issue a final warning. God will send an angel with the message to refuse the beast's mark or suffer eternal consequences in the lake of fire. God gives people free will and the ability to choose. Either take the mark of the beast to save your life but lose your soul and go to hell, or get killed to save your soul and go to heaven.

> **Luke 17:33** *Whosoever shall seek to save his life shall lose it; and whosoever shall lose his life*

shall preserve it.

Revelation 14:9** Then **a third angel followed them, saying with a loud voice, "If anyone worships the beast and his image, and receives his mark on his forehead or on his hand, 10 "he himself shall also drink of the wine of the wrath of God, which is poured out full strength into the cup of His indignation. He shall be tormented with fire and brimstone** in the presence of the holy angels and in the presence of the Lamb. 11 **"And the smoke of their torment ascends forever and ever; and they have no rest day or night, who worship the beast and his image, and whoever receives the mark of his name."

The torments for taking the mark of the beast begin almost immediately with the first bowl judgment of God's wrath. There is an adverse biological reaction to the mark of the beast, and everyone who took the mark will get covered with loathsome and malignant sores and skin ulcers.

Revelation** 16:1 Then I heard a loud voice from the s for temple saying to the seven angels, "Go and pour out the bowls of the wrath of God on the earth." 2 **So the first went and poured out his bowl upon the earth, and a foul and loathsome sore came upon the men who had the mark of the beast and those who worshiped his image.

That description has similarities to the COVID injection, which has resulted in millions of adverse reactions, and many otherwise healthy people have just dropped dead suddenly after taking the shot. The similarities only demonstrate how the world is being conditioned and set up to take the mark of the beast.

Sudden Death Syndrome in young vaccinated athletes is a global phenomena

The harlot church, all the global religions that helped the Antichrist come to power and sold their souls to the Devil like a prostitute, will be rejected, hated, robbed, and killed by the ten kings who rule the beast system. These political leaders will burn down what remains of religion, except the worship of Satan and the Antichrist.

> ***Revelation 17:16 "And the ten horns which you saw on the beast, these will hate the harlot, make her desolate and naked, eat her flesh and burn her with fire."***

Second Coming of Christ

The Jews who mourned at the abomination in the temple and got sealed by the angel with the inkhorn that we saw earlier *(Ezekiel 9:2-7)* will see Jesus at the end of the tribulation and mourn when they see him whom they pierced; they will believe in Christ and receive salvation. Jesus, the Apostle John, and the prophet Zechariah all prophesied about that moment.

> ***Matthew 24:30** "Then the sign of the Son of Man will appear in heaven, and **then all the tribes of the earth will mourn, and they will see the Son of Man coming on the clouds of heaven with power***

and great glory.

Revelation 1:7 *Behold, He is coming with clouds,* ***and every eye will see Him, even they who pierced Him. And all the tribes of the earth will mourn because of Him.*** *Even so, Amen.*

Zechariah 12:8 *"In that day* ***the LORD will defend the inhabitants of Jerusalem****; the one who is feeble among them in that day shall be like David, and the house of David shall be like God, like the Angel of the LORD before them.9 "It shall be in that day* ***that I will seek to destroy all the nations that come against Jerusalem.*** *10 "And* ***I will pour on the house of David and on the inhabitants of Jerusalem the Spirit of grace and supplication; then they will look on Me whom they pierced. Yes, they will mourn for Him as one mourns for his only son, and grieve for Him as one grieves for a firstborn.***

The primary purpose of God in the tribulation is to save the Jewish people and judge the nations. God always has redemption and reconciliation in his plans, and by the end of the tribulation at the second coming, all Israel will be saved.

Romans 11:25 *For I do not desire, brethren, that you should be ignorant of this mystery, lest you should be wise in your own opinion, that* ***blindness in part has happened to Israel until the fullness of the Gentiles has come in. 26 And so All Israel will be saved,*** *as it is written: "The Deliverer will come out of Zion, And He will turn away ungodliness from Jacob; 27 For this is My covenant with them, When I take away their sins."*

Ezekiel 20:40 *"For on My holy mountain, on the mountain height of Israel," says the Lord GOD,* ***"there All the house of Israel, all of them in the land,***

*shall serve Me; there I will accept them, and there I will require your offerings and the firstfruits of your sacrifices, together with all your holy things. 41 "I will accept you as a sweet aroma when I bring you out from the peoples **and gather you out of the countries where you have been scattered; and I will be hallowed in you before the Gentiles.***

Return of Christ

We saw the antichrist ride onto the scene on a white horse with a bow as a fake Christ. When Jesus Christ appears, it is with majestic glory, riding on a white horse. He is faithful and true, He is the word of God, and tens of thousands of saints' ride behind him.

*Revelation 19:11 Now I saw heaven opened, and behold, **a white horse. And He who sat on him was called Faithful and True, and in righteousness He judges and makes war. 12 His eyes were like a flame of fire, and on His head were many crowns**. He had a name written that no one knew except Himself. 13 He was clothed with a robe dipped in blood, and **His name is called The Word of God. 14 And the armies in heaven, clothed in fine linen, white and clean, followed Him on white horses.***

*Jude 1:14 Now Enoch, the seventh from Adam, prophesied about these men also, saying, **"Behold, the Lord comes with ten thousands of His saints, 15 "to execute judgment on All**, to convict **All** who are ungodly among them of **All** their ungodly deeds which they have committed in an ungodly way, and of **All** the*

> *harsh things which ungodly sinners have spoken against Him."*

Just the brilliance of Christ's appearance is enough to destroy Satan, the Antichrist, the false prophet, and all the world's armies. A sword, the word of God, proceeds from his mouth, and he judges the world with his word.

> **2 Thessalonians 2:8** *And then the lawless one will be revealed,* **whom the Lord will consume with the breath of His mouth and destroy with the brightness of His coming.**

> **Revelation 19:15 Now out of His mouth goes a sharp sword, that with it He should strike the nations.** *And He Himself will rule them with a rod of iron.* **He Himself treads the winepress of the fierceness and wrath of Almighty God. 16 And He has on His robe and on His thigh a name written: KING OF KINGS AND LORD OF LORDS.**

Christ's judgment is dealt swiftly to the Antichrist and false prophet, and they get immediately cast alive in the lake of fire.

> **Revelation 19:19 And I saw the beast [Antichrist], the kings of the earth, and their armies,** *gathered together to make war against Him who sat on the horse and against His army. 20* **Then the beast was captured, and with him the false prophet** *who worked signs in his presence, by which he deceived those who received the mark of the beast and those who worshiped his image.* **These two were cast alive into the lake of fire burning with brimstone.** *21 And the rest were killed with the sword which proceeded from the mouth of Him who sat on the horse. And all the birds were filled with their flesh.*

Review of beast system

Now that we've seen the prophetic road map and the script of how the events will play out with the Antichrist, the beast system, and the tribulation period, we can work backward from the future to the present to see how we get there. Let's review what we covered to see how the changes we experience today lead to the beast system and the Antichrist tomorrow.

1). Government (Revelation 13, 17, 18). There will be a global government with a tyrannical dictator, the Antichrist, who will rule the world. The world gets parsed into ten regions with ten kings ruling under the dictator. There will be no independent sovereign countries and no human or civil rights. The world will get tracked, monitored, and dominated by a murderous fascist police state in a digital concentration camp. There will be one centralized global Government, military, banking system, and religion under the power of the most vicious tyrant ever to live, the incarnation of Satan. The Antichrist gains power through deception, military intimidation, political cunning and assassinations, sorcery, and miraculous signs. But once he has total control, the raging Satanic beast unleashes hell on earth.

2). Finance (Revelation 13, 18). The Government controls the world's finances in an dictatorial fascist state. The elite globalists and oligarchs control every corporation, business, product, service, and bank under the Antichrist. There will be no physical paper money or coins because anything that is not digital can't be monitored and tracked. The only legal way to buy or sell is to take the Beast's number or name implanted on the right hand or forehead. The mark will likely be a programmable digital identification system linked to bank accounts, credit, and a social scoring system. Every legal transaction will be monitored and controlled by algorithms and artificial intelligence. The penalty for not taking the mark is no access to the financial system and death. Undoubtedly, there will be an underground bartering system; violators will get killed if caught. But a small remnant will survive the tribulation period without taking the mark of the Beast.

3). Harlot church (Revelation 17). The world's religions will consolidate into one to worship Satan and the Antichrist. There will be an ecumenical movement to "coexist," which will turn into forced compliance to worship the Antichrist. The leaders of the world's religions will push their followers into submission to the Antichrist state religion, which could include agendas like Satan worship, gay, transgender, pedophilia, abortion, climate change, wars, fascism, etc. The leaders of the world's religions will be drunk with the blood of the saints who have faith in Jesus

Spirit of Antichrist is here

Agents of Satan are always at work inside the church to deceive the naive; church attendance does not make anyone safe from deception. The apostle John tells us that we are in the last hour, and the spirit of the Antichrist is already in the world. Satan is actively moving around the world to build the ten-horn kingdom so he can give it to the Antichrist whenever the restrainer gets removed.

> *1 John 2:18 Little children, **it is the last hour; and as you have heard that the Antichrist is coming, even now many antichrists have come, by which we know that it is the last hour.** 19 They went out from us, but they were not of us; for if they had been of us, they would have continued with us; but they went out that they might be made manifest, that none of them were of us.*

> *1 John 4:1 Beloved, do not believe every spirit, but test the spirits, whether they are of God; because **many false prophets have gone out into the world**. 2 By this you know the Spirit of God: Every spirit that confesses that Jesus Christ has come in the flesh is of God, 3 **and every spirit that does not confess that Jesus Christ has come in the flesh is not of God. And this is the spirit of the Antichrist, which you have heard was coming, and is now already in the world.***

Only in the last few decades has the technology been available to have a global surveillance and financial system to monitor and control every sale and purchase of every transaction of every person on the earth. The three-legged beast system is forming with politicians, clergy, global elites, technology, international corporations, and organizations, and we are eyewitnesses.

What can we do about the things that are coming? We should be a restraining force that battles in intercessory prayer to hold back the powers of darkness and the Beast system from coming forward. We should also recognize how the stage is getting set, the actors and props that are falling into place, and we should be watchmen warning and proclaiming Christ to others while there is time.

End Times deception

When we see the evil and cruelty men will inflict on the world during the tribulation, it's hard to imagine how humanity can sink to such demonic levels. Why did all the people of Sodom and Gomorrah give themselves to Homosexuality? Why did Israel kill their babies to worship Molech? Why do people do the same things today and celebrate it with pride parades? Evil spirits do not die; they go from generation to generation and from person to person. The demons of sexual perversion went from Sodom and Gomorrah to San Francisco. The demons Jesus cast out are still around today, looking for a host body to call home.

Your master is who you obey. Whenever people give themselves to homosexuality, pornography, drug abuse, false religions, or other vices, they become slaves to those demons. **Evil spirits seek to fulfill their lusts vicariously through a human host**. They seek to steal, kill, and destroy mankind and have dominion over God's creation. Your master is who you obey.

Without realizing it, people become slaves to the demonic forces they serve. If they give their bodies to commit lewd acts, addictions, and destructive lifestyles, they may be under the influence or control of those evil spirits.

> **Romans 6:16** Do you not know that **to whom you present yourselves slaves to obey, you are that one's slaves whom you obey, whether of sin leading to death, or of obedience leading to righteousness?**

> **Ephesians 2:1-2** And you He made alive, who were dead in trespasses and sins, in which **you once walked according to the course of this world, according to the prince of the power of the air [Satan], the spirit who now works in the sons of disobedience,**

Jesus warned believers to guard against being deceived by false prophets. Religious deception is catastrophic because it can take a soul to Hell. The worst thing that can happen is to think we have the truth and are right with God and end up in Hell.

> **Matthew 7:21 "Not everyone who says to Me, 'Lord, Lord,' shall enter the kingdom of heaven**, but he who does the will of My Father in heaven. 22 "Many will say to Me in that day, 'Lord, Lord, have we not prophesied in Your name, cast out demons in Your name, and done many wonders in Your name?' 23 "And then I will declare to them, 'I never knew you; depart from Me, you who practice lawlessness!'**

Deception is the only end-time sign that is purely mental or spiritual. Outside forces can influence and affect our actions, but deception has to do with our thought processes. Satan wants to infiltrate our minds and lead us astray from Christ. And Satan can and will use religious leaders, cults, and institutional denominations, aka the harlot church.

The main targets of Satan and all his minions are the pastors and preachers who influence large groups of people. Satan can be overly religious, infiltrating churches and pretending to be an Angel of light. He also owns men who have sold their souls. They are Satan's apostles, prophets, and ministers who preach a different Jesus, a different gospel, and have a different spirit.

> **2 Corinthians 11:3-4** *But I fear, lest somehow,* ***as the serpent [Satan] deceived Eve by his craftiness, so your minds may be corrupted from the simplicity that is in Christ. For if he who comes preaches another Jesus whom we have not preached, or if you receive a different spirit which you have not received, or a different gospel which you have not accepted you may well put up with it!***

> **2 Corinthians 11:13-15** *For such are* ***false apostles, deceitful workers, transforming themselves into the apostles of Christ. And no marvel; for Satan himself is transformed into an angel of light. Therefore, it is no great thing if his ministers also be transformed as the ministers of righteousness;*** *whose end shall be according to their works.*

The Holy Spirit clearly says that in later times, some will abandon the faith because they follow deceiving spirits and things taught by demons. Such teachings come through hypocrites without conscience, false prophets, and teachers. They will support attacks on traditional marriages and promote every form of sexual immorality and perversion. They will weaponize the food supply, banning real meat and vegetables in favor of lab-grown meat and eating bugs in the name of climate change. They control the masses using fake science, psychology, and earth worship.

1 Timothy 4:1 The Spirit clearly says that in later times some will abandon the faith and follow deceiving spirits and things taught by demons. 2 Such teachings come through hypocritical liars, *whose consciences have been seared as with a hot iron. 3* ***They forbid people to marry and order them to abstain from certain foods****, which God created to be received with thanksgiving by those who believe and who know the truth.* NIV

Revelation 2:14 *"But I have a few things against you, because* ***you have there those who hold the doctrine*** *[teaching]* ***of Balaam, who taught*** *Balak to put a stumbling block before the children of Israel,* ***to eat things sacrificed to idols, and to commit sexual immorality****. 15 "Thus you also have those who hold* ***the doctrine of the Nicolaitans, which thing I hate.*** *16 'Repent, or else I will come to you quickly and will fight against them with the sword of My mouth.*

Revelation 2:20 *"Nevertheless* ***I have a few things against you, because you allow that woman Jezebel, who calls herself a prophetess, to teach and seduce My servants to commit sexual immorality and eat things sacrificed to idols****. 21 "And I gave her time to repent of her sexual immorality, and she did not repent. 22* ***"Indeed I will cast her into a sickbed, and those who commit adultery with her into great tribulation****, unless they repent of their deeds. 23 "I will kill her children with death,* ***and all the churches shall know that I am He who searches the minds and hearts. And I will give to each one of you according to your works.***

Ratio of False Prophets

The apostle Peter also prophesied how, among God's people, false prophets and teachers would bring in destructive heresies. Peter refers to Israel's history to point out how false prophets find influence over the people of God.

> **2 Peter 2:1** But **there were also false prophets among the people [Israel], even as there will be false teachers among you, who will secretly bring in destructive heresies,** even denying the Lord who bought them, and bring on themselves swift destruction.

One familiar example is when Elijah challenged the prophets of Baal to a contest, saying the God who answers by fire is God. So, 450 prophets of Baal and 400 of Asherah responded to his challenge. That makes the Old Testament percentage of false prophets to true prophets of God 850 to 1. Today, thanks to YouTube and social media, the proportion of false prophets compared to true prophets is much bigger than that and is increasing daily.

> **1 Kings 18:19** "Now therefore, send and gather all Israel to me on Mount Carmel, the **four hundred and fifty prophets of Baal, and the four hundred prophets of Asherah, who eat at Jezebel's table.**"

The story should be familiar; the false prophets cried, prayed, and cut themselves all day without results. Elijah stepped forward and said a short prayer, and fire fell from heaven, consuming the sacrifice. He immediately called for the execution of the prophets of Baal, according to the Law of Moses.

> **1 Kings 18:40** And Elijah said to them, **"Seize the prophets of Baal! Do not let one of them escape!" So, they seized them; and Elijah brought them down to the Brook Kishon and executed them there.**

> ***Deuteronomy 13:5** "But that prophet or that dreamer of dreams shall be put to death, because he has spoken in order to turn you away from the LORD your God.*

The 450 prophets of Baal, the pagan male deity, were killed. But somehow, the 400 prophets of Asherah, the pagan female goddess, escaped. That may have been because they were employees of Jezebel, who swore she would kill Elijah in revenge for the execution of the prophets of Baal.

Also, note that the spirit that animated Jezebel was active when John wrote the book of Revelation and is active today. The demons behind Jezebel and Asherah that drove male priest to castrate, emasculate, and feminize themselves, making them submissive to dominant women, are prevailing today and growing in power. Those same demonic spirits are the driving force behind the homosexual, transgender, and gender confusion movements today. There is nothing new under the sun; the same devils create the same cycles of depravity from generation to generation.

That group of 400 prophets reappeared, and again, they confronted one man, Micaiah, a prophet of God. Ahab, the king of Israel, was Jezebel's hen-pecked husband. He hated Micaiah because he always prophesied against him, as Elijah did. The world hates true prophets *(Luke 6:26)*, but Micaiah stood firm against the crowd of 400 false prophets.

> ***1 Kings 22:5-8*** *Also Jehoshaphat said to the king of Israel, "Please inquire for the word of the LORD today."* **Then the king of Israel gathered the prophets together, about four hundred men**, *and said to them, "Shall I go against Ramoth Gilead to fight, or shall I refrain?" So, they said, "Go up, for the Lord will deliver it into the hand of the king." And Jehoshaphat said,* **"Is there not still a prophet of the LORD here, that we may inquire of Him?"** *So, the king of Israel said to Jehoshaphat,* **"There is still one man,**

> *Micaiah the son of Imlah, by whom we may inquire of the LORD; but I hate him, because he does not prophesy good concerning me, but evil."* And Jehoshaphat said, "Let not the king say such things!"

Influence by spirits

The next scene provides unique insights into how spiritual deception and lies get spread through religious communities. Micaiah shares a vision of heaven where **God assigns one spirit to move the 400 prophets to lie and deceive**. Those 400 prophets were sincerely deceived; they believed they prophesied by the Spirit of God, but one lying spirit spoke through each of them, and they were completely unaware of it.

> *1 Kings 22:19-23 Then Micaiah said, "Therefore hear the word of the LORD: I saw the LORD sitting on His throne, and all the host of heaven standing by, on His right hand and on His left. "And the LORD said,* **'Who will persuade Ahab to go up, that he may fall at Ramoth Gilead?'** *So, one spoke in this manner, and another spoke in that manner.* **"Then a spirit came forward and stood before the LORD, and said, 'I will persuade him.'** *"The LORD said to him, 'In what way?' So he said,* **'I will go out and be a lying spirit in the mouth of all his prophets.'** *And the LORD said, 'You shall persuade him, and also prevail. Go out and do so.' "Therefore look!* **The LORD has put a lying spirit in the mouth of all these prophets of yours**, *and the LORD has declared disaster against you."*

We can see the same type of deception that happened with the Apostle Peter. One moment, Jesus tells him he received revelations directly from God the Father. Moments later, Jesus rebuked Satan, who was speaking through Peter. If that could happen to Peter, it only demonstrates the need for our dependence on God to protect us from spiritual deception.

> ***Matthew 16:15-17** He said to them, "But who do you say that I am?"* ***Simon Peter*** *answered and said, "You are the Christ, the Son of the living God." Jesus answered and said to him,* ***"Blessed are you, Simon Bar-Jonah, for flesh and blood has not revealed this to you, but My Father who is in heaven.***
>
> ***Matthew 16:22-23*** *Then* ***Peter*** *took Him aside and began to rebuke Him, saying, "Far be it from You, Lord; this shall not happen to You!" But* ***He turned and said to Peter, "Get behind Me, Satan! You are an offense to Me, for you are not mindful of the things of God, but the things of men."***

Towards the end of his life, an older, wiser Peter recounted his experience on the mount where Jesus became transfigured before him, James, and John. Jesus became more brilliant than the noonday sun, and Moses and Elijah were speaking with Jesus. Then God the Father spoke from heaven and said this is my beloved Son, in whom I am well pleased. Everything that happened that day could not be more legitimate and reliable; Peter saw the actual, literal Jesus and heard God the Father speaking from heaven.

Yet, Peter says we have something "more sure" and credible than his personal experiences, which is, the written word of God. Peter says no prophecy of scripture comes from personal or special interpretation, not by human will, but men moved by the Holy Spirit spoke from God. In other words, **God's word takes precedence over all personal experiences, revelations, dreams, and interpretations**. If something disagrees or does not align with all the scriptures taken in their proper context, it is false and should be rejected and avoided at all costs.

> ***2 Peter 1:16*** *For* ***we did not follow cunningly devised fables*** *when we made known to you the power and coming of our Lord Jesus Christ,* ***but were eyewitnesses of His majesty***. *17 For He received*

*from God the Father honor and glory when such **a voice came to Him from the Excellent Glory: "This is My beloved Son, in whom I am well pleased." 18 And we heard this voice which came from heaven when we were with Him on the holy mountain. 19 And so we have the prophetic word confirmed** [a more sure word of prophecy, KJV], which you do well to heed as a light that shines in a dark place, until the day dawns and the morning star rises in your hearts; 20 **knowing this first, that no prophecy of Scripture is of any private interpretation, 21 for prophecy never came by the will of man, but holy men of God spoke as they were moved by the Holy Spirit**.*

The Apostle Paul was vehemently brutal in his stance. He pronounced a curse against anyone, be it man, angel, or himself, who would in any way alter, modify, or change the gospel of Jesus Christ from the original message preached by Jesus and the apostles.

***Galatians 1:6** I marvel that **you are turning away** so soon from Him who called you in the grace of Christ, **to a different gospel,** 7 which is not another; but there are some who trouble you and want to pervert the gospel of Christ. 8 But even if we, or an angel from heaven, preach any other gospel to you than what we have preached to you, let him be accursed. 9 As we have said before, so now I say again, if anyone preaches any other gospel to you than what you have received, let him be accursed.*

Internet Prophets

The birth of the internet opened Pandora's box for unvetted, unfiltered, and unaccountable free agents of religious banter. Whether good or bad ministries, the floodgates opened, and unfortunately, we saw a rise in New Age, occult, sexual perversion, and heresy masquerade as Christianity. The same internet door for faithful, Bible-based, godly ministries with integrity is being silenced and de-platformed by artificial intelligence and algorithms that only allows approved words and narratives.

But the cat is out of the bag, and we have experienced an ever-increasing deluge of self-proclaimed prophets and spiritual leaders with new home-spun revelations fabricated from their carnal minds or demonic influence from outside the boundaries of the scriptures. We also see spaghetti prophets who keep throwing predictions against the wall, hoping that something will stick. All this leads naive souls away from the authentic Christ to the imposters and deceivers. These false prophets ruin the church's credibility, giving unbelievers and skeptics a reason to mock and damage the cause of Christ. But these are the types of false prophets that Jesus said would come in the end times.

However, this writer disagrees with the Calvinists and cessationists, who say the supernatural gifts of the Holy Spirit have ceased and died with the last apostle. Some cessationists teach against the miraculous power of the Holy Spirit in the church and slander Christians with different opinions. Some like to post videos of the worst examples of religious frauds and paint all Pentecostals and Charismatics as demon-possessed, crazed lunatics. For the record, many godly Pentecostals are Bible-based, with integrity, and they also reject heresy, fraud, and bizarre behavior, test everything by the word of God, and pray for discernment. We vehemently uphold and defend the position that all the supernatural gifts of the Holy Spirit will function in the church until the rapture of the church.

So, until the rapture, people need discernment by the Holy Spirit as to what is from the Spirit of God and the Devil because both are active today. The safe, controlling, and fearful position is to institutionally eliminate or ban the Spiritual gifts and say that everything supernatural is from Satan. The Scribes and Pharisees tried that trick with Jesus, but it didn't work. Jesus didn't tolerate it and put them in their place.

> **Matthew 12:28** *[Jesus speaking] "But if **I cast out demons by the Spirit of God, surely the kingdom of God has come upon you.** ... 31 "Therefore I say to you, every sin and blasphemy will be forgiven men, but **the blasphemy against the Spirit will not be forgiven men. 32 "Anyone who speaks a word against the Son of Man, it will be forgiven him; but whoever speaks against the Holy Spirit, it will not be forgiven him, either in this age or in the age to come.***

> **2 Timothy 3:1** *This know also, that in the last days perilous times shall come. 2 For men shall be lovers of their own selves ... 5 **Having a form of godliness, but denying the power thereof: from such turn away.***

From the first sermon on the day of Pentecost, Peter proclaimed that in the last days, God will pour out his spirit on all flesh, meaning every born-again, Spirit-filled believer. And each believer has the potential to prophesy, have visions, and dream dreams. But it is not a disorderly free-for-all; there is divine order by the Holy Spirit who distributes and oversees spiritual gifts in the church *(1 Corinthians 12 & 14)*. Notice how Peter quoted from Joel and includes the portion of prophecy that takes this promise up to the time of the sun darkening and the moon turning to blood on the great Day of the Lord. That rendering of Joel was intentional; the supernatural gifts of the Holy Spirit will manifest in the church until the dispensation of the church is over on the Day of the Lord.

> **Acts 2:17** *And it shall come to pass **in the last days, saith God, I will pour out of my Spirit upon all flesh**: and your sons and your daughters shall **prophesy**, and your young men shall see **visions**, and*

*your old men shall **dream dreams**: 18 And on my servants and on my handmaidens, **I will pour out in those days of my Spirit; and they shall prophesy: 19 I will show wonders in heaven above and signs in the earth beneath: Blood and fire and vapor of smoke. 20 The sun shall be turned into darkness, And the moon into blood, Before the coming of the great and awesome day of the LORD.***

If we accept the premise that the Holy Spirit is available to all believers and the Spirit distributes gifts to each one according to his will *(1 Corinthians 12:4-11)*, then we have a lot of wheat, chaff, and tares to sift through *(Matthew 13:24-33)*. One of the gifts of the Spirit is the discerning of spirits, the ability to recognize truth and error, fake and genuine, the Holy Spirit, and demonic spirits. We live in times of spiritual extremes; the spiritual atmosphere is getting polarized, the believers separate from sin and cleave to God, and the wicked are becoming more public and aggressive in their evil deeds.

In the church, we have seen how the new age, occult, homosexuality, and sexual perversion changed from being tolerated to being accepted, then promoted, and now are openly persecuting anyone who dares to speak against it. Many so-called churches mock and blaspheme God with their blatant public sins: drag queens, child molestations, homosexuality, fornication, drugs and alcohol, pornography, abortion, astrology, grave soaking, fake healers, greed and financial schemes, the list is endless. We have tens of millions of self-proclaimed prophets on social media and the internet who are detached from Biblical truth, accountability, and reality.

Many churches compete with Hollywood in their Sunday morning rock show slash Broadway productions and are primarily concerned about counting nickels and noses.

They see souls drowning in an ocean of sin and despair and offer them a glass of water! They should be throwing them the lifesaver, the gospel of Jesus Christ. Worldly wisdom and entertainment cannot save anyone. A watered-down, lukewarm gospel will produce watered-down lukewarm Christians.

> ***Galatians 6:7 Do not be deceived: God cannot be mocked. A man reaps what he sows. 8 The one who sows to please his sinful nature, from that nature will reap destruction; the one who sows to please the Spirit, from the Spirit will reap eternal life.***

Discernment is the key to knowing the difference between good and evil, truth and error. In the end times, there will be floods of lies, strong delusions, deceptions, false narratives, and propaganda that will saturate the entire planet so that people will believe unbelievable lies: black is white, white is black, boys are girls, girls are boys, there are 20,000 genders, masks and shuts downs for 15 days to slow the spread, etc. you get the idea.

> ***Isaiah 5:20 Woe to those who call evil good, and good evil; Who put darkness for light, and light for darkness; Who put bitter for sweet, and sweet for bitter!*** *21 Woe to those who are wise in their own eyes, And prudent in their own sight!*

> ***2 Thessalonians 2:9*** *The coming of the lawless one [Antichrist] is according to the working of Satan, with all power, signs,* ***and lying wonders, 10 and with all unrighteous deception among those who perish, because they did not receive the love of the truth, that they might be saved. 11 And for this reason God will send them strong delusion, that they should believe the lie,*** *12 that they all may be condemned who did not believe the truth but had*

pleasure in unrighteousness.

Spiritual winds

We saw how Peter got the revelation from God the Father that Jesus was the Christ and then switched to having Satan speak directly through him. How is that possible? How vulnerable are we to such influences? Even worse, demonic manifestations will significantly increase in the end times, with leaders teaching demonically inspired messages from the pulpits of the "Christian" churches. The following verses will help us understand how that could happen. Remember how one lying spirit spoke through 400 prophets in Micaiah's time? That was a mild breeze compared to the demonic hurricane yet to come.

> ***1 Timothy 4:1-2** Now **the Spirit speaks expressly, that in the latter times some shall depart from the faith, giving heed to seducing spirits, and doctrines of devils; Speaking lies in hypocrisy;** having their conscience seared with a hot iron.*

In the previous verses, we see two types of spirits: the Holy Spirit of God and seducing spirits; the same word for "spirit" is used for the Holy Spirit and the other spirits. Let's read Strong's Concordance definition of the Greek word for spirit, pneuma.

> **Spirit – Greek = pneuma,** a current of air, i.e., breath (blast) or a breeze, a spirit, angel, demon, or (divine) God, Christ's spirit, the Holy Spirit: ghost, life, spirit.

In the original Greek, pneuma is interchangeable between Spirit, breath, and breeze. The same is true with the Hebrew language in the Old Testament, we see the Spirit of God in the second verse of the Bible; the Hebrew word for Spirit is ruwach.

> ***Genesis 1:1-2*** *In the beginning God created the heaven and the earth. And the earth was without form, and void; and darkness was upon the face of the deep. And **the Spirit of God** moved upon the face of the waters.*

Let's read the Strong's Concordance definition of the Hebrew word for spirit, ruwach.

> **Spirit - Hebrew = ruwach,** wind; breath, a sensible (or even violent) exhalation; spirit, spiritual, tempest, whirlwind

So, the picture we get is that spirits are like winds, powerful unseen forces that can influence, control and destroy unsuspecting people. A young and naive Peter could be blown by the Holy Spirit one moment and by Satan the next moment. Jesus describes people who become born of the Spirit as being like winds, moved about in different directions by the unseen hand of God.

> ***John 3:6-8*** *"That which is born of the flesh is flesh, and* ***that which is born of the Spirit is spirit.*** *"Do not marvel that I said to you, 'You must be born again.'* ***"The wind blows where it wishes, and you hear the sound of it, but cannot tell where it comes from and where it goes. So is everyone who is born of the Spirit."***

We don't see spiritual beings but see and feel their effects like the unseen wind. We see the destructive force of hurricanes and tornadoes as evidence of the power of the wind that moves and breaks things. The best example of the movement of the Holy Spirit was on the Day of Pentecost when the Holy Spirit blew like a mighty wind on the disciples, which continues to blow to this day. Some flow with the current of the Holy Spirit, and others are either oblivious or fight against it.

> ***Acts 2:1-4*** *When the Day of Pentecost had fully come, they were all with one accord in one place.* ***And suddenly there came a sound from heaven, as of a rushing mighty wind, and it filled the whole***

house where they were sitting. Then there appeared to them divided tongues, as of fire, and one sat upon each of them. **And they were all filled with the Holy Spirit** *and began to speak with other tongues, as the Spirit gave them utterance.*

Moved by winds

People are like sailboats, blown about by every wind or spirit that catches their sails. We wonder how and why people do the things they do. How could parents change their child's God-given gender and surgically mutilate their child? How could men dress like women and read Bible stories to Sunday school children? We could give an unending list of those types of questions. The answer is simple: They get swept away in the demonic winds of influence, secular, pagan, and religious. And those winds are rapidly picking up to hurricane speed as we approach the worst time in human history, the great tribulation.

> *Ephesians 4:11-14 that we should no longer be children,* **tossed to and fro and carried about with every wind of doctrine***, by the trickery of men, in the cunning craftiness of deceitful plotting,*

> *Jude 1:11-13 Woe to them!* **For they have gone in the way of Cain [murder], have run greedily in the error of Balaam for profit, and perished in the rebellion of Korah***. These are spots in your love feasts, while they feast with you without fear, serving only themselves. They are clouds without water,* **carried about by the winds;** *late autumn trees without fruit, twice dead, pulled up by the roots;* **raging waves of the sea,** *foaming up their own shame; wandering stars for whom is reserved the blackness of darkness forever.*

Whose voice, is it?

Another way influences come is by voices, not audible, but in the inner ear of our mind or soul. Whether we realize it or not, spiritual beings surround us, and a great cloud of witnesses is above us *(Hebrews 12:1)*. God designed us to talk with him and not just audibly in prayer. God is a Spirit, and He can speak to our inner man with the word of God, by the Holy Spirit, and through our conscience. But our spiritual antennas also pick up other voices, not from God, and those voices try to lead us astray. Jesus said my sheep know my voice and the voice of a stranger (Satan); they will not follow.

> ***John 10:1-5*** *"Most assuredly, I say to you, he who does not enter the sheepfold by the door, but climbs up some other way, the same is a thief and a robber. "But **he who enters by the door is the shepherd of the sheep. "To him the doorkeeper opens, and the sheep hear his voice; and he calls his own sheep by name and leads them out. "And when he brings out his own sheep, he goes before them; and the sheep follow him, for they know his voice. "Yet they will by no means follow a stranger, but will flee from him, for they do not know the voice of strangers."***

> ***John 10:27*** *"My sheep hear My voice, and I know them, and they follow Me.*

> ***John 18:37*** *Pilate therefore said to Him, "Are You a king then?" Jesus answered, "You say rightly that I am a king. For this cause I was born, and for this cause I have come into the world, that I should bear witness to the truth. **Everyone who is of the truth hears My voice.**"*

Jesus said My sheep know my voice. The Greek word for voice is phone. Nothing could be more relevant for our times; people are entirely dependent on and addicted to cell phones and technology. The big question is, whose voice do we allow to come through our phones? Cell phones and technology will have a significant role in the end times because of GPS tracking, monitoring, digital banking, digital identification, and passports, which are used for conditioning behavior and transitioning us to submit to the beast system.

One end-time prophecy is getting fulfilled in a unique way using cell phones. Paul said that in the last days, perilous times would come, and men would be "lovers of themselves." **People are lovers of "them selfies."** Selfies are an example of narcissism or self-love. In Greek mythology, Narcissus saw his reflection in the water and became so obsessed and transfixed on himself that he could not move and stared at himself until he died. Self-love is the opposite of God's love, which is a sacrificial love towards others, even enemies.

> *2 Timothy 3:1 But know this, that in the last days perilous times will come: 2 **For men will be lovers of themselves**, lovers of money, boasters, proud, blasphemers, disobedient to parents, unthankful, unholy,*

Just walk into any public place, and you'll see people in groups, not talking or looking at each other, but each with their faces buried in a screen. There's a trap built into our digital devices: all those pictures go up to the internet cloud and are stored with a record of every search, video, post, and text we do. Data is the new gold in the beast system; the world's biggest companies are information and tech companies. When the beast system wants to show its teeth, it will weaponize all that information against us.

Also, social media and all the apps combined with artificial intelligence and algorithms are programmed to make us addicted and dependent on our devices. Artificial intelligence tries to influence and manipulate our behavior and sell us narratives. Currently, in China, cell phones are used by the government to monitor and track movements, finances, and every aspect of life. Citizens are required to keep their phones with them at all times, it's like a government identification app. If we thirst to know God's voice and hear from him, there are times that we need the self-control and discipline to turn off all the devices to block out the stranger's voices so we can give all our attention to Jesus and listen and obey his voice.

> **1 Corinthians 14:10 *There are, it may be, so many kinds of voices in the world, and none of them is without signification.***
>
> **Psalms 95:7** *For He is our God, and we are the people of His pasture, And the sheep of His hand.* ***Today, if you will hear His voice: 8 "Do not harden your hearts,*** *as in the rebellion, as in the day of trial in the wilderness,*
>
> **James 1:22 *But be doers of the word, and not hearers only, deceiving yourselves.***

Test the spirits

Many voices surround us; we get bombarded with messages that try to influence our buying habits, political affiliations, relationships, and beliefs. The purpose of those communications is to echo repeatedly in our minds to manipulate and control our behavior. The source of those voices could be human, demonic, or God, and we need to discern which spirit is behind the voice. Remember how Peter got revelation directly from God the Father, and shortly afterward, Satan spoke through Peter to Jesus? Peter was sincerely concerned for Jesus' safety, but the spirit behind his voice was from Satan. We must test the spirits, whether they are of God or the Devil, especially regarding true or false prophets.

> *1 John 4:1 Beloved, **do not believe every spirit, but test the spirits, whether they are of God;** because many false prophets have gone out into the world.*

> *1 John 4:6 We are of God. He who knows God hears us; he who is not of God does not hear us. By this we know **the spirit of truth** and the **spirit of error.***

> *John 16:13-14 Howbeit when **he, the Spirit of truth,** is come, he **will guide you into all truth: for he shall not speak of himself;** but whatsoever he shall hear, that shall he speak: and **he will shew you things to come. He shall glorify me:** for he shall receive of mine, and shall shew it unto you.*

It is not unusual for someone to get hit with attacks of evil thoughts, especially if they are watching the wrong things. But there could be times while reading the Bible or praying, we get attacked by evil thoughts. We must recognize the source; they could be fiery darts or thoughts fired like flaming arrows at our minds by the wicked one, Satan. We are in the battle of the ages, and the greatest spiritual battles in history are coming. Daily, we must put on the spiritual armor God has provided for us, stand our ground without compromise, and persist in standing firm against every spiritual attack.

.

> *Ephesians 6:11 **Put on the whole armor of God, that you may be able to stand against the wiles of the devil.** 12 **For we do not wrestle against flesh and blood, but against principalities, against powers, against the rulers of the darkness of this age, against spiritual hosts of***

wickedness in the heavenly places. 13 Therefore take up the whole armor of God, that you may be able to withstand in the evil day, and having done all, to stand. 14 **Stand therefore, having girded your waist with truth, having put on the breastplate of righteousness, 15 and having shod your feet with the preparation of the gospel of peace; 16 above all, taking the shield of faith with which, you will be able to quench all the fiery darts of the wicked one.** *17* **And take the helmet of salvation, and the sword of the Spirit, which is the word of God;**

Our battle is not with flesh and blood; our warfare and weapons are spiritual. The battlefield is our mind, and we must take every thought captive and make it obedient to Christ, the word of God. We must train our minds to think, ponder, and meditate on the word of God at all times. If we don't fill our minds with God's word, the Devil will fill it with something else.

> **2 Corinthians 10:4** *The weapons we fight with are not the weapons of the world. On the contrary, they have divine power to demolish strongholds. 5* **We demolish arguments and every pretension that sets itself up against the knowledge of God, and we take captive every thought to make it obedient to Christ.** *6 And we will be ready to punish every act of disobedience, once your obedience is complete.*

Stand on the Word of God
The only sure foundation we have to stand on is the word of God. We can't pick and choose the parts we like and don't like. One sign of the end times is that professing believers will turn away from the word of God to fables and other nonsense. That will lead to a spiritual famine from hearing God's word, the bread of life, the manna from heaven. Jesus is the word of God made flesh, so to abandon the word of God is to discontinue having a relationship with Jesus.

> **2 Timothy 4:1 I charge you therefore before God and the Lord Jesus Christ, who will judge the living and the dead at His appearing and His kingdom: 2 Preach the word!** *Be ready in season and out of season. Convince, rebuke, exhort, with all longsuffering and teaching. 3* **For the time will come when they will not endure sound doctrine, but according to their own desires, because they have itching ears, they will heap up for themselves teachers; 4 and they will turn their ears away from the truth, and be turned aside to fables.**
>
> **Amos 8:11** *"Behold,* **the days are coming,"** *says the Lord GOD,* **"That I will send a famine on the land, not a famine of bread, nor a thirst for water, but of hearing the words of the LORD. 12 They shall wander from sea to sea, and from north to east; They shall run to and fro, seeking the word of the LORD, but shall not find it.**

The best defense against spiritual deception is the word of God and prayer. From the Garden of Eden to Jesus in the wilderness, the battle is God's word versus Satan's lies and deception. When we read, study, obey, and live the word of God, we can stand no matter what storms surround us.

> **Matthew 7:24-29 Whosoever heareth these sayings of mine, and doeth them, I will liken him unto a wise man, which built his house upon a rock: And the rain descended, and the floods came, and the winds blew, and beat upon that house; and it fell not: for it was founded upon a rock.** *And every one that heareth these sayings of mine,* **and doeth them not, shall be likened unto a foolish man,** *which built his house upon the sand***: And the rain descended, and the floods came, and the winds blew, and beat upon that house; and it fell: and great was the fall of it.**

The word of God is our daily bread; we need to study and rightly divide it. The chart below shows principles for discerning good and bad Bible preaching and teaching.

Good Preaching	Bad Preaching
Context, Cross reference	Pretext, Twisting Scripture
Preach Christ, Humble, Hidden Life with God	Preach Themselves, Self Exalting and Promoting
Word of God, Cross, Gospel, Evangelism	Self Help, Psychology, Comedy, Politics
Everlasting Gospel, True Every Generation	Earthly Vision, Trendy, Fads, Winds of Doctrine
Whole Counsel of God, Balanced Messages	Single Topic, Narrow Message, Tunnel Vision
Godliness, Holiness	Worldliness, Compromise
Ministry of the Spirit, Reconciliation with God	Ministry of Judgment, Condemnation, Guilt
Called, Sent, Zeal, Spirit Filled	Hirelings, Wrong Motives, Greed, Spiritually Dead
Every Believer Teaches, Makes Disciples, Gifted,	Believers are Spectators, Silent, Sedentary,

Know God, not a religion

Religion cannot save, and professing Christians who are not born again, the lukewarm and backslidden will get swept away with the floods of deception in times of change while the beast system comes to power. These are times to have a close relationship with God and not depend on a denomination, church building, or pastor for salvation. In the exodus from Egypt, crossing the Red Sea, and wilderness wonderings, the children of Israel saw all the miracles that God did, but Moses learned God's ways and character; he talked to God face to face, like a friend. Head knowledge alone is not faith or a relationship with God and cannot save anyone.

> **Ps 103:6** *The LORD executes righteousness and justice for all who are oppressed. 7* **He made known His ways to Moses, His acts to the children of Israel.** *8 The LORD is merciful and gracious, Slow to anger, and abounding in mercy.*

Nobody knew the scriptures better than the Scribes and Pharisees, but Jesus told them their head knowledge could not save them. The religious leaders searched the scriptures but would not come to Jesus, who was the word of God made flesh and standing in front of them. Instead, they persecuted him. We need a personal relationship with Jesus, the word of God, and learn of God's character and ways.

> **John 5:38** *"But* **you do not have His word abiding in you**, *because whom He sent, Him you do not believe. 39* **"You search the Scriptures, for in them you think you have eternal life; and these are they which testify of Me. 40 "But you are not willing to come to Me that you may have life.**

When we read about all the suffering and persecution that the apostle Paul went through, we are amazed at how one man could endure so much and keep charging forward through so much persecution and pain to preach Christ. The answer is simple: he would pay any price to know Christ.

> **Philippians 3:7** *But what things were gain to me, these I have counted loss for Christ. 8 Yet* **indeed I also count all things loss for the excellence of the knowledge of Christ Jesus my Lord, for whom I have suffered the loss of all things, and count them as rubbish, that I may gain Christ 9 and be found in Him,** *not having my own righteousness, which is from the law, but that which is through faith in Christ, the righteousness which is from God by faith;* **10 that I may know Him and the power of His resurrection, and the**

fellowship of His sufferings, being conformed to His death, 11 if, by any means, I may attain to the resurrection from the dead.

Jeremiah 9:23 This is what the LORD says: "Let not the wise man boast of his wisdom or the strong man boast of his strength or the rich man boast of his riches, 24 **but let him who boasts boast about this: that he understands and knows me, that I am the LORD***, who exercises kindness, justice and righteousness on earth, for in these I delight," declares the LORD.*

When we have Paul's resolve, nothing can separate us from the love of God in Christ. We can go through anything and look forward confidently to the blessed hope of the rapture and meeting Christ in the air, and no Antichrist or Devil can stop it.

Romans 8:37 Yet in all these things **we are more than conquerors through Him who loved us.** *38 For I am persuaded that neither death nor life, nor angels nor principalities nor powers, nor things present nor things to come, 39 nor height nor depth, nor any other created thing, shall be able to separate us from the love of God which is in Christ Jesus our Lord.*

May God, find you watching, counted worthy, and present you faultless to Christ at the rapture when the church meets Jesus in the air.

Luke 21:36 "Watch therefore, and pray always that you may be counted worthy to escape all these things that will come to pass, and to stand before the Son of Man."

Jude 1:24 Now to Him who is able to keep you from stumbling, and to present you faultless Before the presence of His glory with exceeding joy

Call to Action

We are in the end times; our world is changing quickly to line up with Bible prophecy. Jesus said the signs of his return would be like birth pangs, growing globally in intensity and frequency. We are seeing those signs happening weekly in real-time with wars, food shortages, pandemics, shutdowns, and natural disasters, all leading to global tyranny. There will be global persecution of Christians and Jews, and it's not a question of if, but when. There will also be a great falling away from Christ, and we can see it happening already. So-called churches are already becoming sexually immoral, politically woke, and in bed with the government. As more churches go apostate or get shut down, true believers may have to find or create small groups for fellowship. While we have time and freedom, we should study the scriptures, share the gospel, and watch for Jesus to return.

This book is part of a series of studies that all Christians should know and teach. We call it the "toolbox series" because these studies are tools to equip you to share your faith with others. For free resources and study materials, visit our website at **Ears2Hear.online.**

Ears2Hear.online
Free E-books, Audio books, Bibles, resources, links, etc.
Also available on Kindle & Amazon
Search: Tool Box Series Mark England
Email: Ears@Ears2Hear.online

Charts

The following charts are self-explanatory and are all related to the Antichrist and end times prophecy and timelines. They are provided as an extra resource.

	Antichrist's Rise to Power
Rev 12:3	Dragon with 7 heads 10 horns (Dragon holds power)
Rev 13:1	Beast rises from the sea, (multitudes of people)
Rev 17:1,15	Harlot sits on many waters (multitudes of peoples)
Rev 17:3	Harlot sitting on the Beast (allied in power)
Rev 17:8	Beast once was, is not, shall ascend out of the Abyss
Rev 13:2	Dragon gave Beast power, throne, authority
Rev 13:3, 12	Beast fatal wound had been healed
Dan 7:8, 20	Little Horn defeats 3 of the 10 Horns to take power
Dan 7:24	10 Kings, 1 King subdues (puts down) 3 Kings
Rev 17:11	He is the 8th of the 7 (7 horns plus antichrist = 8)
Rev 17:12	10 Horns/10 kings received no kingdom as yet
Rev 17:13,17	10 Horns give power to Beast
Rev 13:4	Dragon gives authority to Beast, who can war against?
Rev 13:5	Beast exercises authority 3.5 years
Dan 7:25	Power given to kill saints for 3.5 years
Rev 11:7	Ascends bottomless pit, makes war with 2 Witnesses
Rev 17:16	Antichrist & 10 horns hate the Harlot and destroy her
Rev 13:7	Power to kill Saints, all kindreds, tongues, nations
Rev 13:14	Image of Beast that was killed yet lives (resurrected)
Rev 13:15-18	Worship the image, take the mark of beast, or die

Dragon = Satan   Harlot = Evil Global Religious System
Beast, Little Horn = Antichrist   Horns = Kings, Political Leaders

	Person & Activities of the Antichrist / Beast
Dan 8:23	He will appear on the scene in the "latter days" of Israel's history
2 Thess. 2:2	He will not appear until the day of the Lord has begun
2 Thess. 2:6-7	His manifestation is being hindered by the Restrainer
2 Thess. 2:3	His appears after an apostacy, departure from faith, and the rapture
Rev 13:1	He is a Gentile, he rises from the sea (sea = Gentile nations Rev 17:15)
Dan 9:26	He rises from Roman empire; rules people who destroyed Jerusalem
Rv 13:1; 17:9	He will be dictator of the last Gentile empire, like a leopard, bear, lion
Dan 7:8,24	He eliminates 3 rulers in his rise to power (from 10 heads down to 7)
Rev 13:1;17:12	He will be a dictator over 7 heads & 10 horns (7 rulers & 10 regions)
Rev 13:8	His influence is worldwide, he will rule over all nations
Dan 8:24	He gains influence by alliances he makes with other nations (Rev 17:12)
Rv 13:3, 17:10	He revives after a mortal headwound, or revives his political career
Dan 8:25	His rise to power comes through a peace program
Dan 7:8,20;8:23	He is intelligent/persuasive/crafty (Ezek. 28:6) rules by consent (Rev 17:13)
Dan 11:36;7:25	He's a dictator, self willed, gains authority thru changing laws/customs
Dan 11:38	His chief interest is might & power
Dan 9:27	As head of a global federation he confirms a 7-year covenant with Israel
Dan 9:27	After 3 ½ years he breaks the covenant,
Dan 9:27	He demands worship as a god (Dan 11:36-37; 2 Thess. 2:4; Rev 13:5)
Ezek. 28:2	He is a blasphemer because he claims deity (Dan 7:25, Rev 13:1, 5-6)
Rev 13:4	He is possessed by Satan, receives his authority (Ezek 28:2, 9-12; Dan 8:25)
2 Thess. 2:3	His claims of power/deity proven by false signs/wonders (2 Thess 2:9-19)
Dan 7:21, 25	This ruler becomes the great adversary of Israel (Dan 8:24; Rev 13:7)
Ezek. 28:7	An alliance against him will contest his authority (Dan 11:40, 42)
Dan 11:42-45	He conquers the middle east, puts tents in the "glorious land" of Israel
Rev 17:3	He rises to power with the help of the Harlot (corrupt religious system)
Rev 17:16-17	He destroys the Harlot religious system to rule unhindered
Dan 8:24-25	He fights Jesus (2 Thess. 2:4; Rev 17:14) and his people (Dan 7:21, 25; Rev 13:7)
Dan 9:25-27	His Satanic activity begins in the middle of trib (Dan 7:25;11:36; Rev13:5)
Ezek. 28:6	His rule ends by God's judgment (Dan 7:22, 26 8:25; 9:27; 11:45; Rev 19:19-20) he wars against Israel, is cast into Lake of Fire (Ezek. 28:8-10; Rev 19:19-20)
2 Thess. 2:8	His army, the nations are judged/destroyed by Christ (Dan 9:22, Rev 11:15)
Dan 7:27	The beast kingdom is conquered, becomes Messianic kingdom & saints

The Rapture / Church	Second Coming / Israel
Believers disappear	Christ appears
Unseen – like a thief	Every eye sees Him
Rapture, over in a moment,	Christ wars & judges nations
Meet the Lord in air	Rules on earth 1,000 years
Christ comes for his Bride	Christ returns with His Bride
Ushers in the tribulation	Ushers in the Millennium
Imminent – no warnings	Preceded by many signs
Message of comfort	Message of judgment
Program for the church	Program for Israel & nations
New Testament only	From Genesis to Revelation
Believers are judged	Nations & Israel are judged
Leaves creation unchanged	Creation is changed
Nations are unaffected	The nations are judged
Israel's covenants unfulfilled	All Israel's covenants fulfilled
No effect on sin in the world	Sin is judged, destroyed
Before the day of wrath	Christ executes God's wrath
Is for believers only	Affects everyone on earth

Names & Titles of the Antichrist

Ps 5:6	The bloody deceitful man	Dan 7:8	The little horn
Ps 10:2-4	The wicked one	Dan 9:26	The prince that shall come
Ps 10:18	The man of the earth	Dan 11:21	The vile person
Ps 52:1	The mighty man	Dan 11:36	The willful king
Ps 55:3	The enemy	Zech 11:16-17	The idol shepherd
Ps 74:8-10	The adversary	2 Thess 2:3	The son of perdition
Ps 111:6	The head of many countries	2 Thess 2:8	The lawless one
Ps 140:1	The violent man	1 Jn 2:22	The antichrist
Isa 10:5-12	The Assyrian	Rev 9:11	The angel of the bottomless pit
Isa 14:2	The king of Babylon	Rev 11:7	The beast
Isa 14:12	The Sun of the morning	Jn 5:23	The one coming in his own name
Isa 16:4-5	The spoiler (Jer 6:26)	Dan 8:23	The king of fierce countenance
Isa 22:25	The nail	Matt 24:15	The abomination of desolation
Isa 25:5	The branch of the terrible ones	Dan 9:27	The desolater
Ezek. 21:25-27	Profane wicked prince of Israel		

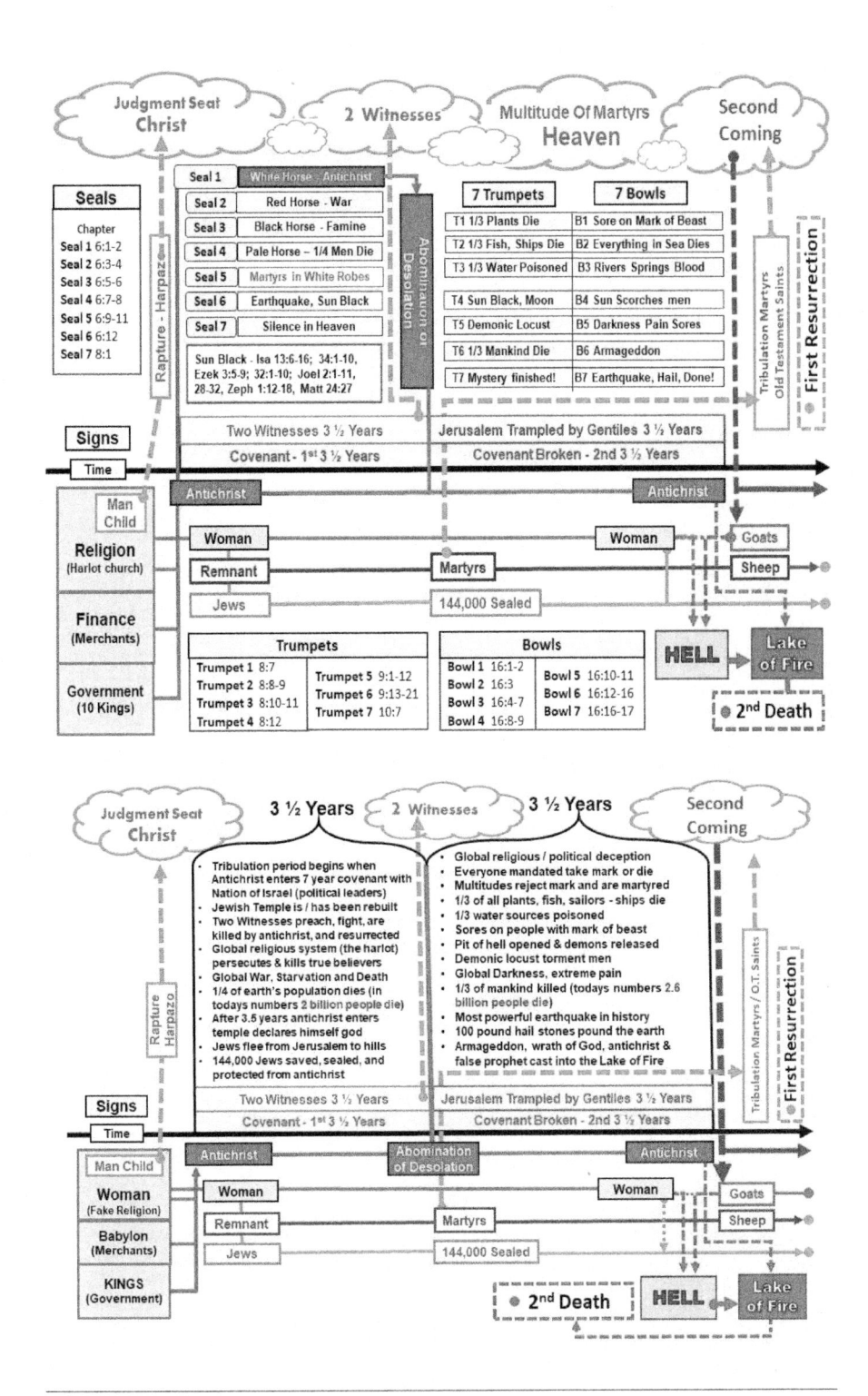

Revelation Timeline Chart

Top Chart

Clouds (Heaven events): Judgment Seat Christ | 2 Witnesses | Multitude Of Martyrs — Heaven | Second Coming

Seals
Chapter
- Seal 1 6:1-2
- Seal 2 6:3-4
- Seal 3 6:5-6
- Seal 4 6:7-8
- Seal 5 6:9-11
- Seal 6 6:12
- Seal 7 8:1

Seal 1	White Horse - Antichrist
Seal 2	Red Horse - War
Seal 3	Black Horse - Famine
Seal 4	Pale Horse – 1/4 Men Die
Seal 5	Martyrs in White Robes
Seal 6	Earthquake, Sun Black
Seal 7	Silence in Heaven

Sun Black - Isa 13:6-16; 34:1-10, Ezek 3:5-9; 32:1-10, Joel 2:1-11, 28-32, Zeph 1:12-18, Matt 24:27

7 Trumpets
- T1 1/3 Plants Die
- T2 1/3 Fish, Ships Die
- T3 1/3 Water Poisoned
- T4 Sun Black, Moon
- T5 Demonic Locust
- T6 1/3 Mankind Die
- T7 Mystery finished!

7 Bowls
- B1 Sore on Mark of Beast
- B2 Everything in Sea Dies
- B3 Rivers Springs Blood
- B4 Sun Scorches men
- B5 Darkness Pain Sores
- B6 Armageddon
- B7 Earthquake, Hail, Done!

Rapture - Harpazo | **Abomination of Desolation** | **Tribulation Martyrs / Old Testament Saints** | **First Resurrection**

Two Witnesses 3 ½ Years | Jerusalem Trampled by Gentiles 3 ½ Years
Covenant - 1st 3 ½ Years | Covenant Broken - 2nd 3 ½ Years

Signs / Time axis

Antichrist — Antichrist

- Man Child
- **Religion** (Harlot church): Woman — Woman — Goats
- Remnant — Martyrs — Sheep
- **Finance** (Merchants): Jews — 144,000 Sealed
- **Government** (10 Kings)

Trumpets
- Trumpet 1 8:7
- Trumpet 2 8:8-9
- Trumpet 3 8:10-11
- Trumpet 4 8:12
- Trumpet 5 9:1-12
- Trumpet 6 9:13-21
- Trumpet 7 10:7

Bowls
- Bowl 1 16:1-2
- Bowl 2 16:3
- Bowl 3 16:4-7
- Bowl 4 16:8-9
- Bowl 5 16:10-11
- Bowl 6 16:12-16
- Bowl 7 16:16-17

HELL → Lake of Fire — 2nd Death

Bottom Chart

Clouds: Judgment Seat Christ | 3 ½ Years | 2 Witnesses | 3 ½ Years | Second Coming

First 3 ½ Years
- Tribulation period begins when Antichrist enters 7 year covenant with Nation of Israel (political leaders)
- Jewish Temple is / has been rebuilt
- Two Witnesses preach, fight, are killed by antichrist, and resurrected
- Global religious system (the harlot) persecutes & kills true believers
- Global War, Starvation and Death
- 1/4 of earth's population dies (in todays numbers 2 billion people die)
- After 3.5 years antichrist enters temple declares himself god
- Jews flee from Jerusalem to hills
- 144,000 Jews saved, sealed, and protected from antichrist

Second 3 ½ Years
- Global religious / political deception
- Everyone mandated take mark or die
- Multitudes reject mark and are martyred
- 1/3 of all plants, fish, sailors - ships die
- 1/3 water sources poisoned
- Sores on people with mark of beast
- Pit of hell opened & demons released
- Demonic locust torment men
- Global Darkness, extreme pain
- 1/3 of mankind killed (todays numbers 2.6 billion people die)
- Most powerful earthquake in history
- 100 pound hail stones pound the earth
- Armageddon, wrath of God, antichrist & false prophet cast into the Lake of Fire

Rapture Harpazo | **Tribulation Martyrs / O.T. Saints** | **First Resurrection**

Two Witnesses 3 ½ Years | Jerusalem Trampled by Gentiles 3 ½ Years
Covenant - 1st 3 ½ Years | Covenant Broken - 2nd 3 ½ Years

Signs / Time axis

Antichrist — Abomination of Desolation — Antichrist

- Man Child
- **Woman** (Fake Religion): Woman — Woman — Goats
- Remnant — Martyrs — Sheep
- **Babylon** (Merchants): Jews — 144,000 Sealed
- **KINGS** (Government)

2nd Death ← HELL → Lake of Fire

Printed in Great Britain
by Amazon